NIST Special Publication 800-37

**National Institute of
Standards and Technology**
Technology Administration
U.S. Department of Commerce

Guide for the Security Certification and Accreditation of Federal Information Systems

Ron Ross
Marianne Swanson
Gary Stoneburner
Stu Katzke
Arnold Johnson

AF394180

INFORMATION SECURITY

Computer Security Division
Information Technology Laboratory
National Institute of Standards and Technology
Gaithersburg, MD 20899-8930

May 2004

U.S. Department of Commerce
Donald L. Evans, Secretary

Technology Administration
Phillip J. Bond, Under Secretary of Commerce for Technology

National Institute of Standards and Technology
Arden L. Bement, Jr., Director

Reports on Computer Systems Technology

The Information Technology Laboratory (ITL) at the National Institute of Standards and Technology (NIST) promotes the U.S. economy and public welfare by providing technical leadership for the Nation's measurement and standards infrastructure. ITL develops tests, test methods, reference data, proof of concept implementations, and technical analyses to advance the development and productive use of information technology. ITL's responsibilities include the development of management, administrative, technical, and physical standards and guidelines for the cost-effective security and privacy of other than national security-related information in federal information systems. The Special Publication 800-series reports on ITL's research, guidelines, and outreach efforts in information system security, and its collaborative activities with industry, government, and academic organizations.

Authority

This document has been developed by the National Institute of Standards and Technology (NIST) in furtherance of its statutory responsibilities under the Federal Information Security Management Act (FISMA) of 2002, Public Law 107-347.

NIST is responsible for developing standards and guidelines, including minimum requirements, for providing adequate information security for all agency operations and assets, but such standards and guidelines shall not apply to national security systems. This guideline is consistent with the requirements of the Office of Management and Budget (OMB) Circular A-130, Section 8b(3), Securing Agency Information Systems, as analyzed in A-130, Appendix IV: Analysis of Key Sections. Supplemental information is provided A-130, Appendix III.

This guideline has been prepared for use by federal agencies. It may also be used by nongovernmental organizations on a voluntary basis and is not subject to copyright. (Attribution would be appreciated by NIST.)

Nothing in this document should be taken to contradict standards and guidelines made mandatory and binding on federal agencies by the Secretary of Commerce under statutory authority. Nor should these guidelines be interpreted as altering or superseding the existing authorities of the Secretary of Commerce, Director of the OMB, or any other federal official.

National Institute of Standards and Technology Special Publication 800-37, 64 pages
(May 2004) CODEN: NSPUE2

Certain commercial entities, equipment, or materials may be identified in this document in order to describe an experimental procedure or concept adequately. Such identification is not intended to imply recommendation or endorsement by the National Institute of Standards and Technology, nor is it intended to imply that the entities, materials, or equipment are necessarily the best available for the purpose.

There are references in this publication to documents currently under development by NIST in accordance with responsibilities assigned to NIST under the Federal Information Security Management Act of 2002. These include: NIST Special Publication 800-53, NIST Special Publication 800-53A, and FIPS 200. The methodologies in this document may be used even before the completion of the aforementioned companion documents. Thus, until such time as each is document is completed, current requirements, guidelines and procedures (where they exist) remain operative. For planning and transition purposes, agencies may wish to closely follow the development of these new documents by NIST. Individuals are also encouraged to review the public draft documents and offer their comments to NIST.

COMMENTS MAY BE SUBMITTED TO THE COMPUTER SECURITY DIVISION,
INFORMATION TECHNOLOGY LABORATORY, NIST, VIA ELECTRONIC MAIL AT SEC-CERT@NIST.GOV
OR VIA REGULAR MAIL AT

100 BUREAU DRIVE (MAIL STOP 8930)
GAITHERSBURG, MD 20899-8930

Acknowledgements

The authors, Ron Ross, Marianne Swanson, Gary Stoneburner, Stu Katzke, and Arnold Johnson of the National Institute of Standards and Technology (NIST) wish to thank their colleagues who reviewed drafts of this document and contributed to its development. The authors also gratefully acknowledge and appreciate the many contributions from the public and private sectors whose thoughtful and constructive comments improved the quality and usefulness of this publication.

Table of Contents

EXECUTIVE SUMMARY

The purpose of this publication is to provide guidelines for the security certification and accreditation of information systems supporting the executive agencies of the federal government. The guidelines have been developed to help achieve more secure information systems within the federal government by:

- Enabling more consistent, comparable, and repeatable assessments of security controls in federal information systems;

- Promoting a better understanding of agency-related mission risks resulting from the operation of information systems; and

- Creating more complete, reliable, and trustworthy information for authorizing officials—to facilitate more informed security accreditation decisions.

Security certification and accreditation are important activities that support a risk management process and are an integral part of an agency's information security program.

Security accreditation is the official management decision given by a senior agency official to authorize operation of an information system and to explicitly accept the risk to agency operations, agency assets, or individuals based on the implementation of an agreed-upon set of security controls. Required by OMB Circular A-130, Appendix III, security accreditation provides a form of quality control and challenges managers and technical staffs at all levels to implement the most effective security controls possible in an information system, given mission requirements, technical constraints, operational constraints, and cost/schedule constraints. By accrediting an information system, an agency official accepts responsibility for the security of the system and is fully *accountable* for any adverse impacts to the agency if a breach of security occurs. Thus, responsibility and accountability are core principles that characterize security accreditation.

It is essential that agency officials have the most complete, accurate, and trustworthy information possible on the security status of their information systems in order to make timely, credible, risk-based decisions on whether to authorize operation of those systems. The information and supporting evidence needed for security accreditation is developed during a detailed security review of an information system, typically referred to as security *certification*. Security certification is a comprehensive assessment of the management, operational, and technical security controls in an information system, made in support of security accreditation, to determine the extent to which the controls are implemented correctly, operating as intended, and producing the desired outcome with respect to meeting the security requirements for the system. The results of a security certification are used to reassess the risks and update the system security plan, thus providing the factual basis for an authorizing official to render a security accreditation decision.

The security certification and accreditation process consists of four distinct phases:

- Initiation Phase;

- Security Certification Phase;

- Security Accreditation Phase; and

- Continuous Monitoring Phase.

Each phase in the security certification and accreditation process consists of a set of well-defined tasks and subtasks that are to be carried out, as indicated, by responsible individuals (e.g., the Chief Information Officer, authorizing official, authorizing official's designated representative, senior agency information security officer, information system owner, information owner, information system security officer, certification agent, and user representatives).

The **Initiation Phase** consists of three tasks: (i) preparation; (ii) notification and resource identification; and (iii) system security plan analysis, update, and acceptance. The purpose of this phase is to ensure that the authorizing official and senior agency information security officer are in agreement with the contents of the system security plan, including the system's documented security requirements, before the certification agent begins the assessment of the security controls in the information system.

The **Security Certification Phase** consists of two tasks: (i) security control assessment; and (ii) security certification documentation. The purpose of this phase is to determine the extent to which the security controls in the information system are implemented correctly, operating as intended, and producing the desired outcome with respect to meeting the security requirements for the system. This phase also addresses specific actions taken or planned to correct deficiencies in the security controls and to reduce or eliminate known vulnerabilities in the information system. Upon successful completion of this phase, the authorizing official will have the information needed from the security certification to determine the risk to agency operations, agency assets, or individuals—and thus, will be able to render an appropriate security accreditation decision for the information system.

The **Security Accreditation Phase** consists of two tasks: (i) security accreditation decision; and (ii) security accreditation documentation. The purpose of this phase is to determine if the remaining known vulnerabilities in the information system (after the implementation of an agreed-upon set of security controls) pose an acceptable level of risk to agency operations, agency assets, or individuals. Upon successful completion of this phase, the information system owner will have: (i) authorization to operate the information system; (ii) an interim authorization to operate the information system under specific terms and conditions; or (iii) denial of authorization to operate the information system.

The **Continuous Monitoring Phase** consists of three tasks: (i) configuration management and control; (ii) security control monitoring; and (iii) status reporting and documentation. The purpose of this phase is to provide oversight and monitoring of the security controls in the information system on an ongoing basis and to inform the authorizing official when changes occur that may impact on the security of the system. The activities in this phase are performed continuously throughout the life cycle of the information system.

Completing a security accreditation ensures that an information system will be operated with appropriate management review, that there is ongoing monitoring of security controls, and that reaccreditation occurs periodically in accordance with federal or agency policy and whenever there is a significant change to the system or its operational environment.

CHAPTER ONE

INTRODUCTION

THE NEED FOR SECURITY CERTIFICATION AND ACCREDITATION

The E-Government Act (Public Law 107-347) passed by the one hundred and seventh Congress and signed into law by the President in December 2002 recognized the importance of information security[1] to the economic and national security interests of the United States. Title III of the E-Government Act, entitled the Federal Information Security Management Act (FISMA), requires each federal agency to develop, document, and implement an agency-wide information security program to provide information security for the information and information systems[2] that support the operations[3] and assets of the agency, including those provided or managed by another agency, contractor, or other source. The information security program must include:

- Periodic assessments of risk, including the magnitude of harm that could result from the unauthorized access, use, disclosure, disruption, modification, or destruction of information and information systems that support the operations and assets of the agency;

- Policies and procedures that are based on risk assessments, cost-effectively reduce information security risks to an acceptable level, and ensure that information security is addressed throughout the life cycle of each agency information system;

- Subordinate plans for providing adequate information security for networks, facilities, information systems, or groups of information systems, as appropriate;

- Security awareness training to inform personnel (including contractors and other users of information systems that support the operations and assets of the agency) of the information security risks associated with their activities and their responsibilities in complying with agency policies and procedures designed to reduce these risks;

- Periodic testing and evaluation of the effectiveness of information security policies, procedures, practices, and security controls[4] to be performed with a frequency depending on risk, but no less than annually;

- A process for planning, implementing, evaluating, and documenting remedial actions to address any deficiencies in the information security policies, procedures, and practices of the agency;

- Procedures for detecting, reporting, and responding to security incidents; and

- Plans and procedures to ensure continuity of operations for information systems that support the operations and assets of the agency.

---

[1] Information security is the protection of information and information systems from unauthorized access, use, disclosure, disruption, modification, or destruction in order to provide confidentiality, integrity, and availability.

[2] An information system is a discrete set of information resources organized expressly for the collection, processing, maintenance, use, sharing, dissemination, or disposition of information.

[3] Agency operations include such things as mission, functions, image, and reputation.

[4] Security controls are the management, operational, and technical controls (i.e., safeguards or countermeasures) prescribed for an information system to protect the confidentiality, integrity, and availability of the system and its information.

FISMA, the Paperwork Reduction Act of 1995, and the Information Technology Management Reform Act of 1996 (Clinger-Cohen Act), explicitly emphasize a risk-based policy for cost-effective security. In support of and reinforcing this legislation, the Office of Management and Budget (OMB) through Circular A-130, Appendix III, *Security of Federal Automated Information Resources*, requires executive agencies[5] within the federal government to:

- ***Plan*** for security;

- ***Ensure*** that appropriate officials are assigned security responsibility;

- ***Review*** the security controls in their information systems; and

- ***Authorize*** system processing prior to operations and periodically thereafter.

These management responsibilities presume that responsible agency officials understand the risks and other factors that could adversely affect their missions. Moreover, these officials must understand the current status of their security programs and the security controls planned or in place to protect their information and information systems in order to make informed judgments and investments that appropriately mitigate risk to an acceptable level. The ultimate objective is to conduct the day-to-day operations of the agency and to accomplish the agency's stated missions with what OMB Circular A-130, Appendix III, defines as *adequate security*, or security commensurate with risk, including the magnitude of harm resulting from the unauthorized access, use, disclosure, disruption, modification, or destruction of information.

Security *accreditation* [6] is the official management decision given by a senior agency official to authorize operation of an information system and to explicitly accept the risk to agency operations, agency assets, or individuals[7] based on the implementation of an agreed-upon set of security controls. The senior agency official should have the authority to oversee the budget and business operations of the information system. Required by OMB Circular A-130, Appendix III, security accreditation provides a form of quality control and challenges managers and technical staffs at all levels to implement the most effective security controls possible in an information system, given mission requirements, technical constraints, operational constraints, and cost/schedule constraints. By accrediting an information system, an agency official accepts responsibility for the security of the system and is fully *accountable* for any adverse impacts to the agency if a breach of security occurs. Thus, responsibility and accountability are core principles that characterize security accreditation.

The assessment of risk and the development of system security plans are two important activities in an agency's information security program that directly support security accreditation and are required by FISMA and OMB Circular A-130, Appendix III. Risk assessments influence the development of the security controls for information systems and generate much of the information needed for the associated system security plans. Risk assessments can be accomplished in a variety of ways depending on the specific needs of the agency. Some agencies may choose to assess risk informally. Other agencies may choose to employ a more formal and structured approach. In either case, the assessment of risk is a process that should be incorporated

---

[5] An executive agency is: (i) an Executive Department specified in 5 U.S.C., Section 101; (ii) a Military Department specified in 5 U.S.C., Section 102; (iii) an independent establishment as defined in 5 U.S.C., Section 104(1); and (iv) a wholly owned government corporation fully subject to the provisions of 31 U.S.C., Chapter 91.

[6] Security *accreditation* is synonymous with security *authorization*; the terms are used interchangeably in this special publication.

[7] Risks to individuals may include, but are not limited to, loss of the privacy to which individuals are entitled under law.

into the system development life cycle. At a minimum, documentation should be produced that describes the process employed and the results obtained. System security plans provide an overview of the information security requirements and describe the security controls in place or planned for meeting those requirements. System security plans can include as references or attachments, other important security-related documents (e.g., risk assessments, contingency plans, incident response plans, security awareness and training plans, information system rules of behavior, configuration management plans, security configuration checklists, privacy impact assessments, system interconnection agreements) produced as part of an agency's information security program.[8]

In addition to risk assessments and system security plans, security assessments play an important role in security accreditation. It is essential that agency officials have the most complete, accurate, and trustworthy information possible on the security status of their information systems in order to make timely, credible, risk-based decisions on whether to authorize operation of those systems. The information and supporting evidence needed for security accreditation is developed during a detailed security review of an information system, typically referred to as security *certification*. Security certification is a comprehensive assessment of the management, operational, and technical security controls[9] in an information system, made in support of security accreditation, to determine the extent to which the controls are implemented correctly, operating as intended, and producing the desired outcome with respect to meeting the security requirements for the system. The results of a security certification are used to reassess the risks and update the system security plan, thus providing the factual basis for an authorizing official to render a security accreditation decision.

By accrediting an information system, an agency official accepts the risks associated with operating the system and the associated implications on agency operations, agency assets, or individuals. Completing a security accreditation ensures that an information system will be operated with appropriate management review, that there is ongoing monitoring of security controls, and that reaccreditation occurs periodically in accordance with federal or agency policy and whenever there is a significant change to the system or its operational environment.[10]

1.1 PURPOSE AND APPLICABILITY

The purpose of this publication is to provide guidelines for the security certification and accreditation of information systems supporting the executive agencies of the federal government. The guidelines have been developed to help achieve more secure information systems within the federal government by:

---

[8] NIST Special Publications 800-18, 800-30, 800-34, 800-47, 800-50, 800-61, and 800-70 respectively, provide guidance on system security plans, risk management and risk assessments, contingency planning, information system interconnections, security awareness and training, incident response planning, and security configuration checklists.

[9] Management controls are the safeguards or countermeasures that focus on the management of risk and the management of information system security. Operational controls are the safeguards or countermeasures that primarily are implemented and executed by people (as opposed to systems). Technical controls are the safeguards or countermeasures that are primarily implemented and executed by the information system through mechanisms contained in the hardware, software, or firmware components of the system.

[10] Examples of significant changes to an information system that should be reviewed for possible reaccreditation include but are not limited to: (i) installation of a new or upgraded operating system, middleware component, or application; (ii) modifications to system ports, protocols, or services; (iii) installation of a new or upgraded hardware platform or firmware component, or (iv) modifications to cryptographic modules or services. Changes in laws, directives, policies, or regulations, while not always directly related to the information system, can also potentially affect the security of the system and trigger a reaccreditation action.

- Enabling more consistent, comparable, and repeatable assessments of security controls in federal information systems;

- Promoting a better understanding of agency-related mission risks resulting from the operation of information systems; and

- Creating more complete, reliable, and trustworthy information for authorizing officials—to facilitate more informed security accreditation decisions.

The guidelines provided in this special publication are applicable to all federal information systems other than those systems designated as national security systems as defined in 44 U.S.C., Section 3542.[11] The guidelines have been broadly developed from a technical perspective so as to be complementary to similar guidelines for national security systems. This publication provides augmented, updated security certification and accreditation information to federal agencies and will functionally replace Federal Information Processing Standards (FIPS) 102, *Guidelines for Computer Security Certification and Accreditation*, September 1983, when it is rescinded. State, local, and tribal governments, as well as private sector organizations comprising the critical infrastructure of the United States, are encouraged to consider the use of these guidelines, as appropriate.

1.2 SYSTEM DEVELOPMENT LIFE CYCLE

All federal information systems, including operational systems, systems under development, and systems undergoing some form of modification or upgrade, are in some phase of what is commonly referred to as the system development life cycle.[12] There are many activities occurring during the life cycle of an information system dealing with the issues of cost, schedule, and performance. In addition to the functional requirements levied on an information system, security requirements must also be considered. When fully implemented, the information system must be able to meet its functional requirements and do so in a manner that is secure enough to protect agency operations, agency assets, and individuals.

In accordance with the provisions of FISMA, agencies are required to have an agency-wide information security program and that program should be effectively integrated into the system development life cycle. For new information systems (or major upgrades to information systems), the security certification and accreditation tasks begin early in the system development life cycle during the initiation, development, and acquisition phases and are important in shaping and influencing the security capabilities of the system. For operational systems and older legacy systems, the certification and accreditation tasks may, by necessity, begin later in the system development life cycle during the operations and maintenance phase and be more costly to implement. In either situation, all of the tasks should be completed to ensure that:

- The information system has received the necessary attention with regard to security; and

- The authorizing official explicitly accepts the risk to agency operations, agency assets, or individuals based on the implementation of an agreed-upon set of security controls.

---

[11] NIST Special Publication 800-59 provides guidance for identifying an information system as a national security system.

[12] There are typically five phases in the system development life cycle of an information system: (i) system initiation; (ii) system development and acquisition; (iii) system implementation; (iv) system operations and maintenance; and (v) system disposal. NIST Special Publication 800-64 provides guidance on the security considerations in the information system development life cycle.

1.3 ORGANIZATION OF THIS SPECIAL PUBLICATION

The remainder of this special publication is organized as follows:

- **Chapter 2** describes the fundamentals of security certification and accreditation and includes: (i) an agency-wide view on cost-effective implementation; (ii) the roles and responsibilities of key participants; (iii) the considerations for determining accreditation boundaries; (iv) an introduction to common security controls; (v) types of accreditation decisions; (vi) requirements for supporting documentation; and (vii) the need for continuous monitoring of security controls.

- **Chapter 3** provides an overview of the different phases of the security certification and accreditation process and includes: (i) a description of the associated tasks and subtasks in each phase; (ii) the responsibilities of various participants in each subtask; (iii) guidance to help explain how to execute each subtask; (iv) supplemental guidance for low-impact information systems; and (v) appropriate references to supporting policies, standards, and guidelines.

- **Supporting appendices** provide more detailed security certification and accreditation-related information and include: (i) general references; (ii) definitions and terms; (iii) acronyms; (iv) summary of tasks and subtasks; and (v) sample accreditation transmittal and decision letters.

CHAPTER TWO

THE FUNDAMENTALS

BASIC CONCEPTS ASSOCIATED WITH SECURITY CERTIFICATION AND ACCREDITATION

The purpose of this chapter is to describe the fundamentals of security certification and accreditation to include: (i) agency-level activities that can promote more cost-effective certification and accreditation processes; (ii) roles and responsibilities of key participants; (iii) approaches for determining accreditation boundaries; (iv) partitioning of security controls to facilitate reuse of assessment results; (v) types of security accreditation decisions; (vi) necessary documentation and supporting materials; and (vii) ongoing activities employed to monitor the effectiveness of security controls.

2.1 SECURITY CERTIFICATION AND ACCREDITATION

While security certification and accreditation are very closely related, they are indeed very distinct activities. Security accreditation is about the acceptance and management of risk—the risk to agency operations, agency assets, or individuals that results from the operation of an information system. Authorizing officials must be able to determine the risk to operations, assets, or individuals and the acceptability of such risk given the mission or business needs of their agencies. Authorizing officials must weigh the appropriate factors and decide to either accept or reject the risk to their respective agencies. To ensure that authorizing officials make credible, risk-based decisions, the following questions must be answered during the security certification and accreditation process:

- Does the potential risk to agency operations, agency assets, or individuals described in the system security plan (or risk assessment) prior to security certification appear to be correct, and if so, would this risk be acceptable?

- Are the security controls in the information system effective in achieving the desired level of protection as defined by the security requirements for the system?

- What specific actions have been taken or are planned to correct any deficiencies in the security controls for the information system and to reduce or eliminate known vulnerabilities—and have resources been allocated to accomplish those actions?

- How do the results of security certification translate into actual agency-level risk and is this risk acceptable?

Security certification directly supports security accreditation by providing authorizing officials with important information necessary to make credible, risk-based decisions on whether to place information systems into operation or continue their current operation. This information is produced by assessing the security controls in the information system to determine the extent to which the controls are implemented correctly, operating as intended, and producing the desired outcome with respect to meeting the security requirements for the system. Security certification can include a variety of assessment methods (e.g., interviewing, inspecting, studying, testing, demonstrating, and analyzing) and associated assessment procedures depending on the depth and breadth of assessment required by the agency.[13]

---

[13] NIST Special Publication 800-53A provides guidance for assessing the security controls in an information system.

The determination as to whether the security controls selected are in fact adequate to meet the security requirements for the information system is made during the initiation phase of the system development life cycle. It is in this phase of the life cycle that security requirements are established, security controls selected, and the authorizing official and senior agency information security officer approve the system security plan.[14] For legacy information systems (i.e., systems that are currently in the operations and maintenance phase of the system development life cycle), the determination of security control adequacy is, once again, accomplished prior to security certification when the system security plan is approved.

Security certification does not include the determination of risk to agency operations, agency assets, or individuals. The determination of program-level or agency-level risk generally requires a broader, more strategic view of the agency than can be obtained from the more technically focused, system-level view of the information system that results from security certification. Authorizing officials or their designated representatives are better positioned to make mission risk determinations based on the known vulnerabilities remaining in the information system after the implementation of an agreed-upon set of security controls. The ultimate decision on the acceptability of such risk is the responsibility of the authorizing official. Authorizing officials or their designated representatives may, when needed, consult other individuals within the agency (e.g., senior agency information security officers, information system owners, information system security officers, or certification agents), at any phase in the certification and accreditation process to obtain advice on the security of the information system. Figure 2.1 illustrates the relationship between information system vulnerabilities and program/agency-level, mission risk.

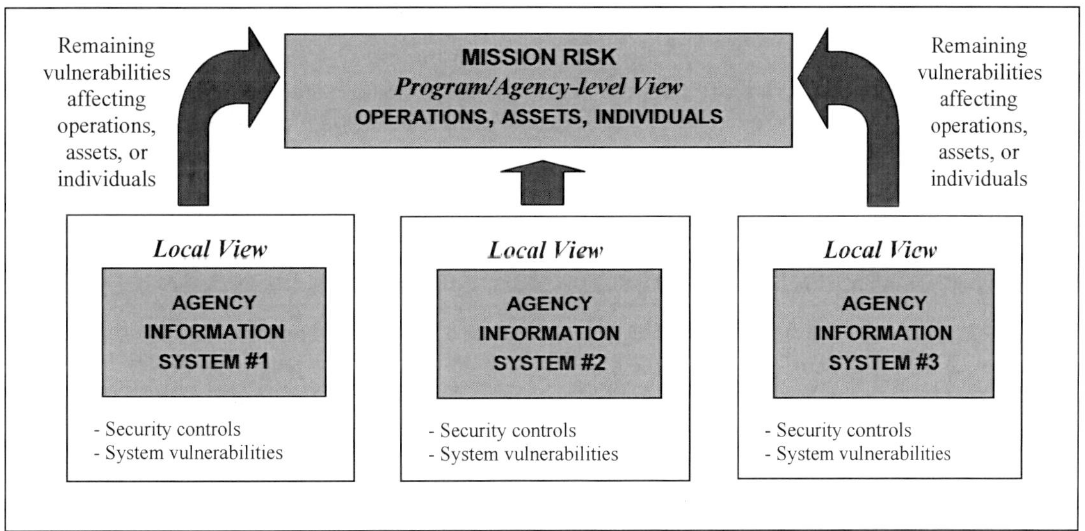

FIGURE 2.1   INFORMATION SYSTEM VULNERABILITIES AND MISSION RISK

Security accreditation is part of a dynamic, ongoing risk management process. An information system is authorized for operation at a specific point in time reflecting the current security state of the system. The inevitable changes to the information system (including hardware, firmware,

---

[14] Security certification and accreditation activities should be closely linked to and be a part of the system development life cycle for the information system. This linkage and integration into the life cycle will ensure that important security-related considerations are included in the design, development, implementation, and operation of the information system.

software and people) and the potential impact those changes may have on agency operations, agency assets, or individuals, require a structured and disciplined process capable of monitoring the effectiveness of the security controls in the information system on an ongoing basis. Thus, the initial security accreditation must be supplemented and reinforced by a continuous monitoring process that: (i) tracks the changes to the information system; (ii) analyzes the security impact of those changes; (iii) makes appropriate adjustments to the security controls and the system security plan; and (iv) reports the security status of the system to appropriate agency officials. The following questions should be answered during the continuous monitoring process:

- Could any of the changes to the information system affect the current, identified vulnerabilities in the system or introduce new vulnerabilities into the system?

- If so, would the resulting risk to agency operations, agency assets, or individuals be unacceptable?

- When will the information system need to be reaccredited in accordance with federal or agency policy?

The successful completion of the security certification and accreditation process provides agency officials with the necessary confidence that the information system has adequate security controls, that any vulnerabilities in the system have been considered in the risk-based decision to authorize processing, and that appropriate plans and funds have been identified to correct any deficiencies in the information system.

An Agency-wide Perspective

When considering the prospect of accrediting agency information systems, it is important to put these activities into perspective with respect to the agency's mission and operational responsibilities. Employing more secure information systems is critical to the success of an agency in carrying out its mission and conducting its day-to-day functions. However, security is only one of many factors that must be considered by agency officials in the design, development, acquisition, operation, and maintenance of information systems. In the end, agencies must have systems that provide a high degree of functionality *and* adequate security so as not to place their respective missions at unacceptable levels of risk.

The increasing costs required to adequately protect agency information systems necessitates an agency-wide view of security to make the costs more manageable.[15] Agencies must consider their entire inventory of information systems when developing appropriate strategies and programs for protecting those systems and managing agency-level risks. The cost of accrediting large numbers of information systems with varying degrees of complexity is a critical issue facing agencies today. The solution to this problem can be found in part, by creating and maintaining an agency-wide information security program that promotes the reuse and sharing of security control development, implementation, and assessment-related information including:

- Employment of standardized security controls and methods for assessing those controls;

- Development of standardized assessment plans, methods and procedures to be used in security certifications and accreditations;

- Adoption, specification, and promulgation of standardized policies, procedures, and documentation for common security program areas (e.g., rules of behavior, system

---

[15] Some agencies may choose to establish an authorization advocate or security certification and authorization organization that manages, coordinates, and oversees all security authorization activities, agency-wide—working with the senior agency information security officer, authorizing officials, and information system owners.

administration, auditing, system monitoring, vulnerability scanning, management of user accounts, configuration management, incident response, contingency planning, and system maintenance);

- Refinement of policies, procedures, and documentation on a system-by-system basis, as needed, by preparing amendments or adding system-specific appendices;

- Adoption, publication, and distribution (preferably in an online database) of agency prescribed or developed security implementation guidance;

- Establishment of a protected central repository, preferably online, for all certification and accreditation documentation, acquisition-related information, risk and vulnerability assessments, compliance surveys, security incident reporting and remediation results, external security audits, and making these easily accessible by appropriate agency personnel; and

- Procurement of agency-wide licenses for automated tools such as vulnerability scanners, online security monitoring tools, audit reduction tools, and certification and accreditation support tools.

Since the cost of security certification and accreditation can be substantial, it is important to leverage the results of previous assessments and audits that have been conducted on an agency's information system or the particular components comprising that system. Several potential sources for consideration include: (i) commercial product testing and evaluation programs;[16] (ii) privacy impact assessments; (iii) physical security assessments; (iv) self-assessments;[17] and (v) internal and external audits.[18] These assessments and audits can support the security certification and accreditation process in two important ways. First, the assessment and audit results can be used to gauge the preparedness of an information system for security certification and accreditation by examining the status of key security controls in the system. Second, the results produced during these assessments and audits can be considered and potentially reused, when appropriate, during the security certification and accreditation process.[19] Bringing in assessment and audit results from multiple sources that the security controls in an information system are implemented correctly, operating as intended, and producing the desired outcome with respect to meeting the security requirements for the system, not only reduces the potential cost of security certification and accreditation but also increases the overall confidence in the final results.

Reuse and sharing of security control development, implementation, and assessment-related information can significantly reduce agency security costs in new acquisitions, certifications and

---

[16] Programs for the testing and evaluation of cryptographic modules and information technology products are available under the NIST Cryptographic Module Validation Program (CMVP) (http://csrc.nist.gov/cryptval), and National Information Assurance Partnership (NIAP) Common Criteria Evaluation and Validation Scheme (CCEVS) (http://niap.nist.gov/cc-scheme), respectively, in accordance with federal and international security standards.

[17] Self-assessments can be conducted using a variety of methodologies including the National Security Agency *INFOSEC Assessment* Methodology (http://www.nsa.gov/isso) and NIST Special Publication 800-26, *Security Self-Assessment Guide for Information Technology Systems* (http://csrc.nist.gov/publications).

[18] The Office of the Inspector General typically conducts internal audits on federal agencies. The General Accounting Office conducts external audits on agency information systems using the *Federal Information System Controls Audit Manual* (http://www.gao.gov).

[19] Previous assessment and audit results should always be reviewed and/or analyzed to determine the extent to which those results are still applicable and accurately reflect the current security state of the information system. Where previous results are deemed not fully applicable or less than current, those areas should be reassessed or the differences so noted for consideration in the final security assessment report.

accreditations of similar information systems, and reaccreditations of existing systems—and can ultimately result in a more consistent application of security solutions, agency-wide.

2.2 ROLES AND RESPONSIBILITIES

The following sections describe the roles and responsibilities of key participants involved in an agency's security certification and accreditation process.[20] Recognizing that agencies have widely varying missions and organizational structures, there may be differences in naming conventions for certification and accreditation-related roles and how the associated responsibilities are allocated among agency personnel (e.g., multiple individuals filling a single role or one individual filling multiple roles[21]). However, the basic functions remain the same. The security certification and accreditation process described in this special publication is flexible, allowing agencies to effectively accomplish the intent of the specific tasks within their respective organizational structures to best manage the risks to agency operations, agency assets, or individuals.

Chief Information Officer

The Chief Information Officer[22] is the agency official responsible for: (i) designating a senior agency information security officer; (ii) developing and maintaining information security policies, procedures, and control techniques to address all applicable requirements; (iii) training and overseeing personnel with significant responsibilities for information security; (iv) assisting senior agency officials concerning their security responsibilities; and (v) in coordination with other senior agency officials, reporting annually to the agency head on the effectiveness of the agency information security program, including progress of remedial actions. The Chief Information Officer, with the support of the senior agency information security officer, works closely with authorizing officials and their designated representatives to ensure that an agency-wide security program is effectively implemented, that the certifications and accreditations required across the agency are accomplished in a timely and cost-effective manner, and that there is centralized reporting of all security-related activities.

To achieve a high degree of cost effectiveness with regard to security, the Chief Information Officer encourages the maximum reuse and sharing of security-related information including: (i) threat and vulnerability assessments; (ii) risk assessments; (iii) results from common security control assessments; and (iv) any other general information that may be of assistance to information system owners and their supporting security staffs. In addition to the above duties, the Chief Information Officer and authorizing officials determine the appropriate allocation of resources dedicated to the protection of the agency's information systems based on organizational priorities. In certain instances, the Chief Information Officer may be designated as the authorizing official for agency-wide general support systems or as a co-authorizing official with other senior officials for selected agency information systems.

---

[20] Agencies may define other significant roles (e.g., systems administrators, facilities managers, system security engineers, and operations managers) to support the security certification and accreditation process. The Office of the Inspector General may also become involved and take on the role of independent auditor in assessing the quality of security certification and accreditation processes.

[21] Caution should be exercised when one individual fills multiples roles in the security certification and accreditation process to ensure that the individual retains an appropriate level of independence and remains free from conflicts of interest.

[22] When an agency has not designated a formal Chief Information Officer position, FISMA requires the associated responsibilities to be handled by a comparable agency official.

Authorizing Official

The *authorizing official* (or designated approving/accrediting authority as referred to by some agencies) is a senior management official or executive with the authority to formally assume responsibility for operating an information system at an acceptable level of risk to agency operations, agency assets, or individuals.[23] Through security accreditation, the authorizing official assumes responsibility and is accountable for the risks associated with operating an information system. The authorizing official should have the authority to oversee the budget and business operations of the information system within the agency and is often called upon to approve system security requirements, system security plans, and memorandums of agreement and/or memorandums of understanding. In addition to authorizing operation of an information system, the authorizing official can also: (i) issue an interim authorization to operate the information system under specific terms and conditions; or (ii) deny authorization to operate the information system (or if the system is already operational, halt operations) if unacceptable security risks exist. With the increasing complexities of agency missions and organizations, it is possible that a particular information system may involve multiple authorizing officials. If so, agreements should be established among the authorizing officials and documented in the system security plan. In most cases, it will be advantageous to agree to a lead authorizing official to represent the interests of the other authorizing officials. The authorizing official has inherent U.S. government authority and, as such, must be a government employee.

Authorizing Official Designated Representative

Due to the breadth of organizational responsibilities and significant demands on time, an authorizing official cannot always be expected to participate directly in the planning and technical meetings that occur during the security certification and accreditation process. The authorizing official's *designated representative* is an individual acting on the authorizing official's behalf in coordinating and carrying out the necessary activities required during the security certification and accreditation of an information system. The authorizing official's designated representative interacts with the senior agency information security officer, information system owner, information system security officer, certification agent, user representative(s), and other interested parties during the security certification and accreditation process. The designated representative can be empowered by the authorizing official to make certain decisions with regard to the planning and resourcing of the security certification and accreditation activities, the acceptance of the system security plan, and the determination of risk to agency operations, agency assets, and individuals. The designated representative may also be called upon to prepare the final security accreditation package, obtain the authorizing official's signature on the security accreditation decision letter, and transmit the accreditation package to the appropriate agency officials. The only activity that cannot be delegated by the authorizing official is the security accreditation decision and the signing of the associated accreditation decision letter (i.e., the acceptability of risk to the agency). If a designated representative is not selected, the authorizing official is responsible for carrying out the activities described above.

Senior Agency Information Security Officer

The *senior agency information security officer* is the agency official responsible for: (i) carrying out the Chief Information Officer responsibilities under FISMA; (ii) possessing professional qualifications, including training and experience, required to administer the information security program functions; (iii) having information security duties as that official's primary duty; and (iv)

---

[23] In some agencies, the senior official and the Chief Information Officer may be co-authorizing officials. In this situation, the senior official approves the operation of the information system prior to the Chief Information Officer.

heading an office with the mission and resources to assist in ensuring agency compliance with FISMA. The senior agency information security officer (or supporting staff member) may also serve as the authorizing official's designated representative. The senior agency information security officer serves as the Chief Information Officer's primary liaison to the agency's authorizing officials, information system owners, and information system security officers.

Information System Owner

The *information system owner*[24] is an agency official responsible for the overall procurement, development, integration, modification, or operation and maintenance of an information system. The information system owner is responsible for the development and maintenance of the system security plan and ensures the system is deployed and operated according to the agreed-upon security requirements. The information system owner is also responsible for deciding who has access to the information system (and with what types of privileges or access rights) and ensures that system users and support personnel receive the requisite security training (e.g., instruction in rules of behavior). The information system owner informs key agency officials of the need to conduct a security certification and accreditation of the information system, ensures that appropriate resources are available for the effort, and provides the necessary system-related documentation to the certification agent.[25] The information system owner receives the security assessment results from the certification agent. After taking appropriate steps to reduce or eliminate vulnerabilities, the information system owner assembles the security accreditation package and submits the package to the authorizing official or the authorizing official's designated representative for adjudication.[26]

Information Owner

The *information owner* is an agency official with statutory or operational authority for specified information and responsibility for establishing the controls for its generation, collection, processing, dissemination, and disposal. The information owner is responsible for establishing the rules for appropriate use and protection of the subject information (e.g., rules of behavior) and retains that responsibility even when the information is shared with other organizations. The owner of the information stored within, processed by, or transmitted by an information system may or may not be the same as the information system owner. Also, a single information system may utilize information from multiple information owners. Information owners should provide input to information system owners regarding the security requirements and security controls for the information systems where the information resides.

Information System Security Officer

The *information system security officer* is the individual responsible to the authorizing official, information system owner, or the senior agency information security officer for ensuring the

---

[24] The role of information system owner can be interpreted in a variety of ways depending on the particular agency and the system development life cycle phase of the information system. Some agencies may refer to information system owners as program managers or business/asset/mission owners.

[25] In some situations, the notification of the need to conduct a security certification and accreditation may come from the senior agency information security officer or authorizing official as they endeavor to ensure compliance with federal or agency policy. The responsibility for ensuring appropriate resources are allocated to the security certification and accreditation effort depends on whether the agency uses a centralized or decentralized funding mechanism.

[26] Depending on how the agency has organized and structured its security certification and accreditation activities, the authorizing official may choose to designate an individual other than the information system owner to compile and assemble the information for the accreditation package. In this situation, the designated individual must coordinate the compilation and assembly activities with the information system owner.

appropriate operational security posture is maintained for an information system or program. The information system security officer also serves as the principal advisor to the authorizing official, information system owner, or senior agency information security officer on all matters (technical and otherwise) involving the security of the information system. The information system security officer typically has the detailed knowledge and expertise required to manage the security aspects of the information system and, in many agencies, is assigned responsibility for the day-to-day security operations of the system. This responsibility may also include, but is not limited to, physical security, personnel security, incident handling, and security training and awareness. The information system security officer may be called upon to assist in the development of the system security policy and to ensure compliance with that policy on a routine basis. In close coordination with the information system owner, the information system security officer often plays an active role in developing and updating the system security plan as well as in managing and controlling changes to the system and assessing the security impact of those changes.

Certification Agent

The *certification agent* is an individual, group, or organization responsible for conducting a security certification, or comprehensive assessment of the management, operational, and technical security controls in an information system to determine the extent to which the controls are implemented correctly, operating as intended, and producing the desired outcome with respect to meeting the security requirements for the system. The certification agent also provides recommended corrective actions to reduce or eliminate vulnerabilities in the information system. Prior to initiating the security assessment activities that are a part of the certification process, the certification agent provides an independent assessment of the system security plan to ensure the plan provides a set of security controls for the information system that is adequate to meet all applicable security requirements.

To preserve the impartial and unbiased nature of the security certification, the certification agent should be in a position that is independent from the persons directly responsible for the development of the information system and the day-to-day operation of the system. The certification agent should also be independent of those individuals responsible for correcting security deficiencies identified during the security certification. The independence of the certification agent is an important factor in assessing the credibility of the security assessment results and ensuring the authorizing official receives the most objective information possible in order to make an informed, risk-based, accreditation decision. The security category of the information system as defined in FIPS 199 should guide the degree of independence of the certification agent. When the potential impact on agency operations, agency assets, or individuals is low, a self-assessment activity may be reasonable and appropriate and not require an independent certification agent. When the potential agency-level impact is moderate or high, certification agent independence is needed and justified.

User Representatives

Users are found at all levels of an agency. Users are responsible for the identification of mission/operational requirements and for complying with the security requirements and security controls described in the system security plan. *User representatives* are individuals that represent the operational interests of the user community and serve as liaisons for that community throughout the system development life cycle of the information system. The user representatives assist in the security certification and accreditation process, when needed, to ensure mission requirements are satisfied while meeting the security requirements and employing the security controls defined in the system security plan.

Delegation of Roles

At the discretion of senior agency officials, certain security certification and accreditation roles may be delegated and if so, appropriately documented. Agency officials may appoint appropriately qualified individuals, to include contractors, to perform the activities associated with any security certification and accreditation role with the exception of the Chief Information Officer and authorizing official. The Chief Information Officer and authorizing official have inherent United States Government authority, and those roles should be assigned to government personnel only. Individuals serving in delegated roles are able to operate with the authority of agency officials within the limits defined for the specific certification and accreditation activities. Agency officials retain ultimate responsibility, however, for the results of actions performed by individuals serving in delegated roles.

2.3   ACCREDITATION BOUNDARIES

One of the most difficult and challenging problems for authorizing officials and senior agency information security officers is identifying appropriate security accreditation boundaries for agency information systems. Accreditation boundaries for agency information systems need to be established before the conduct of initial risk assessments and development of system security plans. Boundaries that are unnecessarily expansive (i.e., including too many hardware, software, and firmware components) make the security certification and accreditation process extremely unwieldy and complex. Boundaries that are unnecessarily limited (i.e., including too few hardware, software, and firmware components) increase the number of security certifications and accreditations that must be conducted and thus drive up the total security costs for the agency. The guidelines in the following sections are provided to assist agencies in defining information system boundaries to strike a balance between the costs and benefits of security certification and accreditation.

Establishing Information System Boundaries

The process of uniquely assigning information resources[27] to an information system defines the security accreditation boundary for that system. Agencies have great flexibility in determining what constitutes an information system (i.e., major application or general support system) and the resulting security accreditation boundary that is associated with that system. If a set of information resources is identified as an information system, the resources should generally be under the same direct management control.[28] Direct management control does not necessarily imply that there is no intervening management. It is quite possible for multiple information systems to be validly considered *subsystems*[29] of a single, larger system provided all of these subsystems fall under the same higher management authority. This situation may arise in many agencies when other than major applications (i.e., minor applications) are coalesced for purposes of security certification and accreditation into a general support system. In addition to the

---

[27] Information resources consist of information and related resources, such as personnel, equipment, funds, and information technology.

[28] Direct management control typically involves budgetary, programmatic, or operational authority and associated responsibility. For new information systems, management control can be interpreted as having budgetary/programmatic authority and responsibility for the development and deployment of the information systems. For information systems currently in the federal inventory, management control can be interpreted as having budgetary/operational authority for the day-to-day operations and maintenance of the information systems.

[29] A subsystem is a major subdivision or component of an information system consisting of information, information technology, and personnel that performs one or more specific functions.

consideration of direct management control, it may also be helpful for agencies to consider if the information resources being identified as an information system:

- Have the same function or mission objective and essentially the same operating characteristics and security needs; and

- Reside in the same general operating environment (or in the case of a distributed information system, reside in various locations with similar operating environments).

While the above considerations may be useful to agencies in determining information system boundaries for purposes of security accreditation, they should not be viewed as limiting the agency's flexibility in establishing common sense boundaries that promote effective information security within the available resources of the agency. Authorizing officials and senior agency information security officers should consult with prospective information system owners when establishing information system and security accreditation boundaries. The process of establishing boundaries for agency information systems and the associated security certification and accreditation implications, is an agency-level activity that should include careful negotiation among all key participants—taking into account the mission/business requirements of the agency, the technical considerations with respect to information security, and the programmatic costs to the agency.

Supplementing the above considerations, FIPS 199, *Standards for Security Categorization of Federal Information and Information Systems*, defines security categories for information systems based on potential impact on organizations or individuals should there be a breach of security—that is, a loss of confidentiality, integrity (including authenticity and non-repudiation), or availability.[30] FIPS 199 security categories can play an important part in defining accreditation boundaries by partitioning the agency's information systems according to the criticality or sensitivity of the systems and the importance of those systems in accomplishing the agency's mission. The partitioning process facilitates the cost-effective application of security controls to achieve adequate security commensurate with the mission/business functions being supported by the respective information systems.

Boundaries for Large and Complex Information Systems

The application of security controls within large and complex information systems, even when using FIPS 199 to categorize those systems, may be cost-prohibitive and technically infeasible for the agency. Accordingly, any attempt to assess the security controls in such systems may also be cost-prohibitive and unrealistic. To make this problem more manageable, authorizing officials should examine the nature of the information systems being considered for security certification and accreditation and the feasibility of decomposing the systems into more manageable components. The decomposition of large and complex systems into multiple components, or subsystems, facilitates the application of the security certification and accreditation process in a more cost-effective manner.

---

[30] Based on the definitions provided in OMB Circular A-130, Appendix III, agencies can associate the different types of information systems and applications with the security categories and impact levels defined in FIPS 199. For example, a major application could be expected to have a potential impact level of moderate or high in its security categorization. A minor application could be expected to have a potential impact level of low or moderate in its security categorization. A general support system could be expected to have a potential impact level of low, moderate, or high in its security categorization depending on the criticality or sensitivity of the system, potential impact of loss, and whether the system is supporting (i.e., hosting) any major applications. Minor applications are typically included (or bundled) within a general support system.

For large and complex information systems, the authorizing official and senior agency information security officer may define subsystem components with established subsystem boundaries. The decomposition into subsystem components should be reflected in the system security plan for that large and complex information system. Each subsystem component is fully described in the system security plan, an appropriate security category assigned in accordance with FIPS 199, and an appropriate set of security controls identified. The extent to which the security controls are implemented correctly, operating as intended, and producing the desired outcome with respect to meeting the security requirements for the information system, can be determined by combining security assessments at the subsystem level and adding system-level considerations. This facilitates a more cost-effective certification and accreditation process by enabling scaling of the effort at the subsystem level in accordance with that subsystem's security category and allowing for reuse of certification results at the system level.

To illustrate a simple example of system decomposition and the resulting subsystems, consider a general support system that contains a system guard that monitors the flow of information between two local area networks. The general support system, in this case, can be partitioned into three subsystem components: (i) local area network Alpha; (ii) local area network Bravo; and (iii) the system guard separating the two networks.[31] When all subsystems within the information system have completed the security certification process, an additional certification is performed on the system-level security controls not covered by the individual subsystem certifications, and the results are bundled together into the accreditation package and presented as evidence to the authorizing official. Figure 2.2 illustrates the concept of information system decomposition and the security certification and accreditation process for a large and complex system.

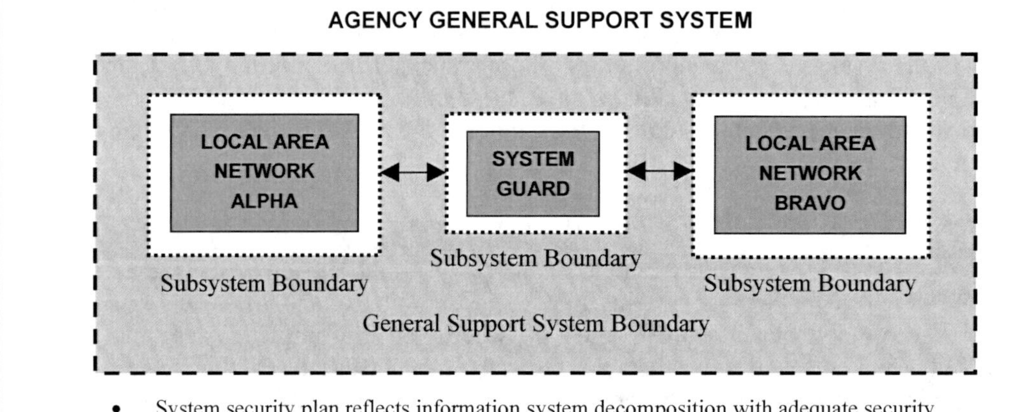

- System security plan reflects information system decomposition with adequate security controls assigned to each subsystem component
- Security assessment methods and procedures tailored for the security controls in each subsystem component and for the combined system level
- Security certification performed on each subsystem component and on system-level controls not covered by subsystem certifications
- Security accreditation performed on the information system as a whole

FIGURE 2.2 DECOMPOSITION OF LARGE AND COMPLEX INFORMATION SYSTEMS

---

[31] Each subsystem component within the information system can be assigned a security categorization in accordance with FIPS 199. The overall security categorization of the information system can be determined by taking the high water mark of the security categorizations of the individual subsystem components.

2.4 COMMON SECURITY CONTROLS

An agency-wide view of the security program facilitates the identification of *common security controls* that can be applied to one or more agency information systems. Common security controls can apply to: (i) all agency information systems; (ii) a group of information systems at a specific site (sometimes associated with the terms site certification/accreditation); or (iii) common information systems, subsystems, or applications (i.e., common hardware, software, and/or firmware) deployed at multiple operational sites (sometimes associated with the terms type certification/accreditation). Common security controls, typically identified during a collaborative agency-wide process with the involvement of the Chief Information Officer, senior agency information security officer, authorizing officials, information system owners, and information system security officers (and by developmental program managers in the case of common security controls for common hardware, software, and/or firmware) have the following properties:

- The development, implementation, and assessment of common security controls can be assigned to responsible agency officials or organizational elements (other than the information system owners whose systems will implement or use those common security controls); and

- The results from the assessment of the common security controls can be used to support the security certification and accreditation processes of agency information systems where those controls have been applied.

Many of the management and operational controls (e.g., contingency planning controls, incident response controls, security training and awareness controls, personnel security controls, and physical security controls) needed to protect an information system may be excellent candidates for common security control status. The objective is to reduce security costs by centrally managing the development, implementation, and assessment of the common security controls designated by the agency—and subsequently, sharing assessment results with the owners of information systems where those common security controls are applied. Security controls not designated as common controls are considered *system-specific controls* and are the responsibility of the information system owner. System security plans should clearly identify which security controls have been designated as common security controls and which controls have been designated as system-specific controls.

2.5 ACCREDITATION DECISIONS

Security accreditation decisions resulting from security certification and accreditation processes should be conveyed to information system owners. To ensure the agency's business and operational needs are fully considered, the authorizing official should meet with the information system owner prior to issuing the security accreditation decision to discuss the security certification findings and the terms and conditions of the authorization. There are three types of accreditation decisions that can be rendered by authorizing officials:

- Authorization to operate;

- Interim authorization to operate; and

- Denial of authorization to operate.

Authorization to Operate

If, after assessing the results of the security certification, the authorizing official deems that the risk to agency operations, agency assets, or individuals is acceptable, an *authorization to operate* is issued for the information system. The information system is authorized without any significant restrictions or limitations on its operation. Although not affecting the security accreditation decision, authorizing officials should take specific actions to reduce or eliminate identified vulnerabilities, where it is cost-effective to do so. The information system owner should establish a disciplined and structured process to monitor the effectiveness of the security controls in the information system and the progress of any corrective actions on a continuous basis. Security reaccreditation occurs at the discretion of the authorizing official when significant changes have taken place in the information system or when a specified time period has elapsed in accordance with federal or agency policy.

Interim Authorization to Operate

If, after assessing the results of the security certification, the authorizing official deems that the risk to agency operations, agency assets, or individuals is unacceptable, but there is an overarching mission necessity to place the information system into operation or continue its operation, an *interim authorization to operate* may be issued. An interim authorization to operate is rendered when the identified security vulnerabilities in the information system resulting from deficiencies in the planned or implemented security controls are significant but can be addressed in a timely manner.[32] An interim authorization provides a limited authorization to operate the information system under specific terms and conditions and acknowledges greater risk to the agency for a specified period of time. The terms and conditions, established by the authorizing official, convey limitations on information system operations.

In accordance with OMB policy, an information system is *not* accredited during the period of limited authorization to operate. The duration established for an interim authorization to operate should be commensurate with the risk to agency operations, agency assets, or individuals associated with the operation of the information system. When the security-related deficiencies have been adequately addressed, the interim authorization should be lifted and the information system authorized to operate. Security reaccreditation occurs at the discretion of the authorizing official when significant changes have taken place in the information system or when a specified time period has elapsed in accordance with federal or agency policy. The time period for reaccreditation is calculated from the date the information system receives its authorization to operate.

The plan of action and milestones submitted by the information system owner is used by the authorizing official to monitor the progress in correcting deficiencies noted during the security certification. In addition to executing the plan of action and milestones, information system owners should also establish a disciplined and structured process to monitor the effectiveness of the security controls in the information system during the period of limited authorization to operate. Monitoring activities should focus on the specific vulnerabilities in the information system identified during the security certification. Significant changes in the security state of the information system that occur during the period of limited authorization to operate should be reported immediately to the authorizing official.

---

[32] Since information system owners are involved in the planning process that establishes timeframes for conducting security certification and accreditation activities, they are in a good position to address security-related deficiencies in a timely manner before the certification and accreditation process begins. Mitigating security vulnerabilities in the information system as soon as possible before the vulnerabilities rise to higher levels of significance or seriousness ensures that the interim authorization to operate remains a viable option. Information systems, especially mission-critical or high-impact systems as described in FIPS 199, should not be operating with significant security vulnerabilities requiring extended remediation time.

Denial of Authorization to Operate

If, after assessing the results of the security certification, the authorizing official deems that the risk to agency operations, agency assets, or individuals is unacceptable, the authorization to operate the information system is denied. The information system is not accredited and should not be placed into operation. If the information system is currently in operation, all activity should be halted. Failure to receive authorization to operate, or an interim authorization to operate, usually indicates that there are major deficiencies in the security controls in the information system. The authorizing official or designated representative should work with the information system owner to revise the plan of action and milestones to ensure that proactive measures are taken to correct the security deficiencies in the information system.

Previous Authorizations

In the event that a new authorizing official is assigned responsibility for the information system, the newly assigned authorizing official should review the current security accreditation package (i.e., accreditation decision, decision rationale, and terms and conditions) and the current status reports from the continuous monitoring process to determine if a reaccreditation action is warranted. If the new authorizing official is willing to accept the currently documented risk, then reaccreditation occurs only when there is a significant change to the information system or when a specified time period has elapsed in accordance with federal or agency policy.

2.6 SUPPORTING DOCUMENTATION

The security *accreditation package* documents the results of the security certification and provides the authorizing official with the essential information needed to make a credible, risk-based decision on whether to authorize operation of the information system. Unless specifically designated otherwise by the Chief Information Officer or authorizing official, the information system owner is responsible for the assembly, compilation, and submission of the security accreditation package. The information system owner receives inputs from the information system security officer, certification agent, and senior agency information security officer during the preparation of the security accreditation package. The security accreditation package contains the following documents:

- Approved system security plan;[33]

- Security assessment report; and

- Plan of action and milestones.

The system security plan, prepared by the information system owner and previously approved by the authorizing official and/or senior agency information security officer, provides an overview of the security requirements for the information system and describes the security controls in place or planned for meeting those requirements. The plan can also contain as supporting appendices or as references, other key security-related documents for the information system such as the risk assessment, privacy impact assessment, contingency plan, incident response plan, configuration management plan, security configuration checklists, and any system interconnection agreements.

The security assessment report, prepared by the certification agent, provides the results of assessing the security controls in the information system to determine the extent to which the controls are implemented correctly, operating as intended, and producing the desired outcome

---

[33] The initial risk assessment, included as an appendix to the system security plan or referenced in the plan, is updated by the information system owner prior to the final assembly of the security accreditation package.

with respect to meeting the system security requirements. The security assessment report can also contain a list of recommended corrective actions.

The plan of action and milestones, which is prepared by the information system owner, describes the measures that have been implemented or planned: (i) to correct any deficiencies noted during the assessment of the security controls; and (ii) to reduce or eliminate known vulnerabilities in the information system. The information system owner submits the final security accreditation package to the authorizing official or designated representative.[34] Figure 2.3 illustrates the key sections of the security accreditation package.

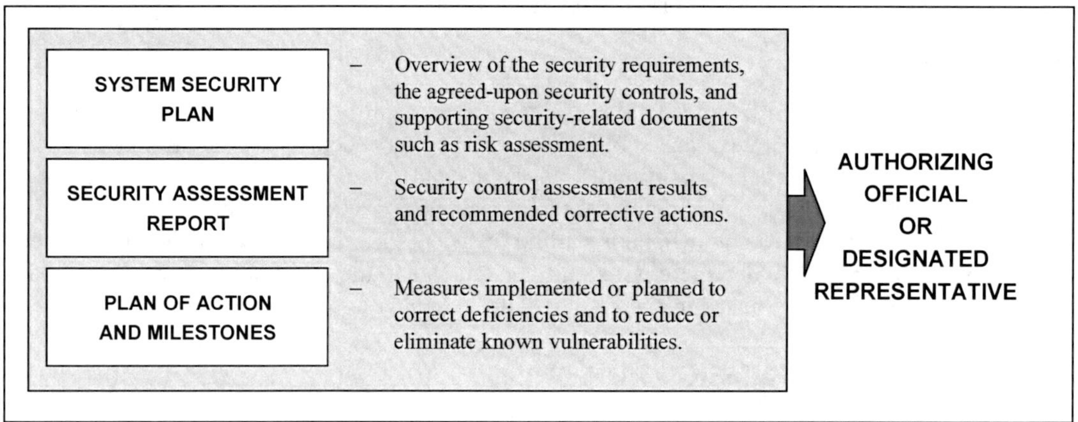

FIGURE 2.3 CONTENTS OF THE SECURITY ACCREDITATION PACKAGE

The security accreditation decision letter transmits the security accreditation decision from the authorizing official to the information system owner. The authorizing official's designated representative prepares the final security accreditation decision letter for the authorizing official with authorization recommendations, as appropriate. The security accreditation decision letter contains the following information:

- Security accreditation decision;

- Supporting rationale for the decision; and

- Terms and conditions for the authorization.

The security accreditation decision letter indicates to the information system owner whether the system is: (i) authorized to operate; (ii) authorized to operate on an interim basis under strict terms and conditions; or (iii) not authorized to operate. The supporting rationale provides the information system owner with the justification for the authorizing official's decision. The terms and conditions for the authorization provide a description of any limitations or restrictions placed on the operation of the information system that must be adhered to by the information system owner. The security accreditation decision letter is attached to the original accreditation package and returned to the information system owner.

Upon receipt of the security accreditation decision letter and accreditation package, the information system owner accepts the terms and conditions of the authorization. The information

---

[34] Security accreditation packages can be submitted in either paper or electronic format. Appropriate measures should be employed to protect the information contained in accreditation packages (electronic or paper format) in accordance with agency policy.

system owner keeps the original security accreditation decision letter and accreditation package on file. The authorizing official and senior agency information security officer also retain copies of the security accreditation decision letter and accreditation package. The contents of security certification and accreditation-related documentation (especially information dealing with information system vulnerabilities) should be: (i) marked and protected appropriately in accordance with agency policy; and (ii) retained in accordance with the agency's record retention policy.

2.7 CONTINUOUS MONITORING

A critical aspect of the security certification and accreditation process is the post-accreditation period involving the continuous monitoring of security controls in the information system over time. An effective continuous monitoring program requires:

- Configuration management and configuration control processes;

- Security impact analyses on changes to the information system; and

- Assessment of selected security controls in the information system and security status reporting to appropriate agency officials.[35]

With regard to configuration management and control, it is important to document the proposed or actual changes to the information system and to subsequently determine the impact of those proposed or actual changes on the security of the system. Information systems will typically be in a constant state of migration with upgrades to hardware, software, or firmware and possible modifications to the surrounding environment where the system resides. Documenting information system changes and assessing the potential impact those changes may have on the security of the system is an essential aspect of continuous monitoring and maintaining the security accreditation.

Realizing that it is not feasible or cost-effective to monitor *all* of the security controls in an information system on a continuous basis, the information system owner should select an appropriate subset of those controls for periodic assessment.[36] The criteria established by the information system owner for selecting which security controls will be monitored and for determining the frequency of such monitoring activity should reflect the agency's priorities and importance of the information system to agency operations, agency assets, or individuals.[37] The authorizing official and the senior agency information security officer should approve the set of security controls that are to be monitored on a continuous basis as well as the monitoring frequency.

The results of continuous monitoring should be documented and reported to the authorizing official and senior agency information security officer on a regular basis. The continuous monitoring results should also be considered with respect to any necessary updates to the system security plan and to the plan of action and milestones, since the authorizing official, senior agency information security officer, information system owner, and certification agent will be using these plans to guide future security certification and accreditation activities. The plan of

---

[35] At the discretion of the agency, the security status reports on agency information systems can be used to help satisfy the FISMA reporting requirement for documenting remedial actions for any security-related deficiencies.

[36] NIST Special Publication 800-53A provides guidance for assessing the security controls in an information system.

[37] FIPS 199 security categorizations should be used to determine agency priorities and importance of information systems.

action and milestones should: (i) report progress made on the current outstanding items listed in the plan; (ii) address vulnerabilities in the information system discovered during the security impact analysis or security control monitoring; and (iii) describe how the information system owner intends to address those vulnerabilities (i.e., reduce, eliminate, or accept the identified vulnerabilities). The monitoring of security controls in the information system continues throughout the system development life cycle. Reaccreditation occurs when there are significant changes to the information system affecting the security of the system or when a specified time period has elapsed in accordance with federal or agency policy.

CHAPTER THREE

THE PROCESS

PHASES AND TASKS ASSOCIATED WITH SECURITY CERTIFICATION AND ACCREDITATION

The security certification and accreditation process consists of four distinct phases: (i) an Initiation Phase; (ii) a Security Certification Phase; (iii) a Security Accreditation Phase; and (iv) a Continuous Monitoring Phase. Each phase consists of a set of well-defined tasks and subtasks that are to be carried out, as indicated, by responsible individuals (e.g., the Chief Information Officer, authorizing official, authorizing official's designated representative, senior agency information security officer, information system owner, information owner, information system security officer, certification agent, and user representatives). The security certification and accreditation activities can be appl[illegible] information system at appropriate phases in the system development life cycle. A[illegible] he activities can be tailored to apply a level of effort and rigor that is most suita[illegible] n system undergoing security certification and accreditation. Fig[illegible] view of the security certification and accreditation process incl[illegible] phase in the process. A summary table of all secu[illegible] nd subtasks and the individuals responsible f[illegible] provided in Appendix D.

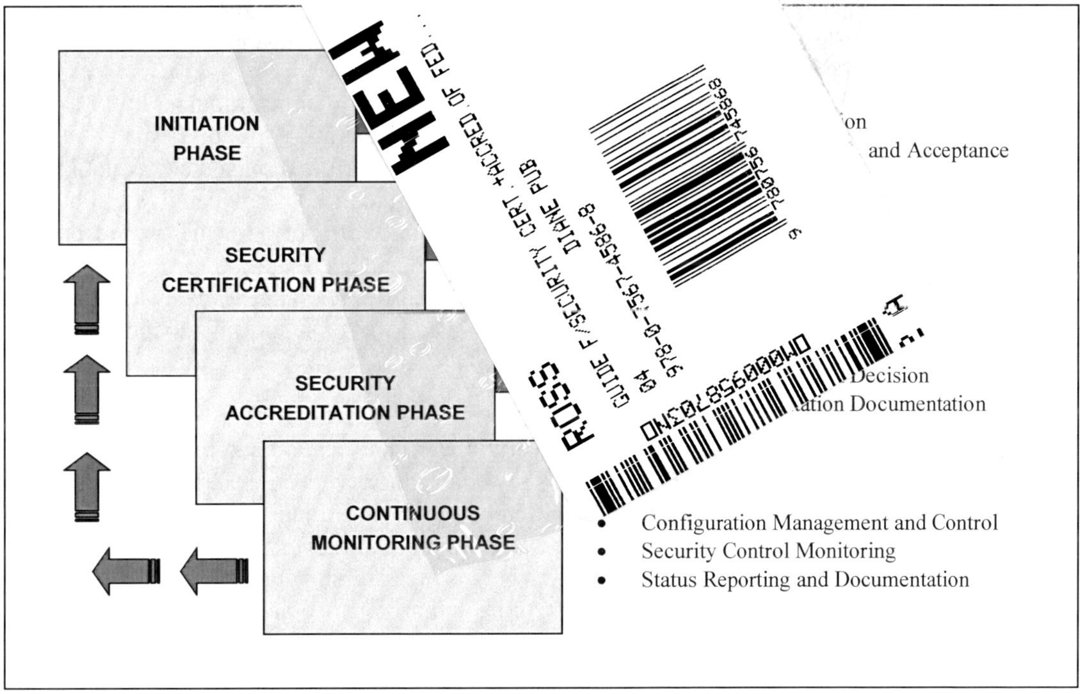

FIGURE 3.1   SECURITY CERTIFICATION AND ACCREDITATION PROCESS

Scalability of the Security Certification and Accreditation Process

There is a general expectation that the level of effort for security certification and accreditation (expressed in terms of degree of rigor and formality) should be scalable to the FIPS 199 security category of the information system. The concept is straightforward—the agency information systems with greater sensitivity and/or criticality have greater potential for adversely affecting agency operations, agency assets, or individuals and therefore demand:

- Greater protection through the application of stronger security controls; and

- Greater scrutiny with regard to the assessment of those security controls to determine the extent to which the controls are implemented correctly, operating as intended, and producing the desired outcome with respect to meeting the security requirements for the system.

The FIPS 199 security category of an information system influences the initial selection of security controls from NIST Special Publication 800-53 and the initial selection of assessment methods and procedures from NIST Special Publication 800-53A. The level of effort applied to the security certification and accreditation tasks and subtasks should be commensurate with the strength of the security controls selected and the rigor and formality of the assessment methods and procedures selected. The tasks outlined in this chapter apply to all FIPS 199 security categories. However, the scalability of the security certification and accreditation process can be applied to low-impact information systems. As stated in FIPS 199:

"For a *low-impact* information system, the loss of confidentiality, integrity, or availability could be expected to have a *limited* adverse effect on agency operations, agency assets, or individuals. A limited adverse effect means that, for example, the loss of confidentiality, integrity, or availability might: (i) cause a degradation in mission capability to an extent and duration that the organization is able to perform its primary functions, but the effectiveness of the functions is noticeably reduced; (ii) result in minor damage to organizational assets; (iii) result in minor financial loss; or (iv) result in minor harm to individuals."

Since the agency-level risk in operating a low-impact information system is minimal, by definition, the level of effort applied to the security certification and accreditation of that system should be commensurate with that level of risk. While all of the certification and accreditation tasks apply to low-impact information systems, supplemental guidance is provided in the subtasks to address the appropriate level of effort (i.e., degree of rigor and formality) for the certification and accreditation process.[38] The scalability of the certification and accreditation process for low-impact systems results in the elimination of the independent certification agent, the incorporation of self-assessment activities, and a reduction in the associated level of supporting documentation.

3.1 INITIATION PHASE

The Initiation Phase consists of three tasks: (i) preparation; (ii) notification and resource identification; and (iii) system security plan analysis, update, and acceptance. The purpose of this phase is to ensure that the authorizing official and senior agency information security officer are in agreement with the contents of the system security plan, including the system's documented security requirements, before the certification agent begins the assessment of the security controls in the information system. The early involvement of the authorizing official and senior agency information security officer, with key participants such as the information system owner, information owner, information system security officer, certification agent, and user representatives, is paramount to the success of the security certification and accreditation effort. A significant portion of the information needed for the Initiation Phase should have been previously generated by the information system owner during: (i) the initial risk assessment; (ii)

---

[38] Supplemental guidance is not provided for all subtasks in the certification and accreditation process. Guidance for scaling the level of effort applied to the development of system security plans, the selection of security controls, and the conduct of risk assessments is beyond the scope of this publication.

the development of the system security plan; and (iii) the conduct of previous assessments (e.g., security testing and evaluation, independent verification and validation, independent audits). For new information systems or systems undergoing major upgrades, this information is typically produced during the initiation phase of the system development life cycle when system requirements are established. For legacy systems currently in the operations and maintenance phase of the system development life cycle, this information is obtained from the most recent system security plans and risk assessments. In most cases, risk assessments and system security plans have been previously reviewed and approved by agency officials. Thus, the subtasks in Task 1 (preparation task) should not require any additional work on the part of the information system owner above and beyond what has already been accomplished as part of the system development life cycle. Rather, the Initiation Phase of the security certification and accreditation process serves as a checkpoint to confirm that the system security plan and risk assessment have been completed. If an information system owner has not completed a risk assessment and a system security plan, those activities should be completed prior to proceeding with the security certification and accreditation process.

TASK 1: PREPARATION

The objective of the preparation task is to prepare for security certification and accreditation by reviewing the system security plan and confirming that the contents of the plan are consistent with an initial assessment of risk.

INFORMATION SYSTEM DESCRIPTION

SUBTASK 1.1:   Confirm that the information system has been fully described and documented in the system security plan or an equivalent document.

RESPONSIBILITY: Information System Owner.[39]

GUIDANCE: A typical system description includes: (i) the name of the information system; (ii) a unique identifier for the information system; (iii) the status of the information system with respect to the system development life cycle; (iv) the name and location of the organization responsible for the information system; (v) contact information for the information system owner or other individuals knowledgeable about the information system; (vi) contact information for the individual(s) responsible for the security of the information system; (vii) the purpose, functions, and capabilities of the information system; (viii) the types of information processed, stored, and transmitted by the information system; (ix) the boundary of the information system for operational authorization (or security accreditation); (x) the functional requirements of the information system; (xi) the applicable laws, directives, policies, regulations, or standards affecting the security of the information and the information system; (xii) the individuals who use and support the information system (including their organizational affiliations, access rights, privileges, and citizenship, if applicable); (xiii) the architecture of the information system; (xiv) hardware and firmware devices (including wireless); (xv) system and applications software (including mobile code); (xvi) hardware, software, and system interfaces (internal and external); (xvii) information flows (i.e., inputs and outputs); (xviii) the

---

[39] Agencies have significant flexibility in assigning security certification and accreditation responsibilities. Some agencies may employ a shared model of responsibility with the senior agency information security officer called upon to assist the information system owner in carrying out security certification and accreditation tasks/subtasks. The delineation and assignment of specific security certification and accreditation responsibilities is handled by agencies on a case-by-case basis in accordance with their organizational structures.

network topology; (xix) network connection rules for communicating with external information systems; (xx) interconnected information systems and unique identifiers for those systems; (xxi) encryption techniques used for information processing, transmission, and storage; (xxii) public key infrastructures, certificate authorities, and certificate practice statements; (xxiii) the physical environment in which the information system operates; and (xxiv) web protocols and distributed, collaborative computing environments (processes, and applications). The level of detail provided in the system security plan depends on the availability of information to the organization preparing the plan and is also commensurate with the FIPS 199 security category of the information system (i.e., the level of detail in the system security plan increases as the potential impact on agency operations, agency assets, or individuals increases). Descriptive information about the information system is typically documented in the system identification section of the system security plan or in some cases, included in attachments to the plan. System identification information can also be provided by reference.

Supplemental Guidance for Low-Impact Systems: *None.*

REFERENCES: NIST Special Publications 800-18, 800-30, or equivalents.

SECURITY CATEGORIZATION

SUBTASK 1.2:   Confirm that the security category of the information system has been determined and documented in the system security plan or an equivalent document.

RESPONSIBILITY: Information System Owner.

GUIDANCE: Consult NIST Special Publication 800-59 to confirm that the information system is other than a national security system. For other than national security systems, FIPS 199 establishes three potential impact levels (low, moderate, and high) for each of the stated security objectives (confidentiality, integrity, and availability) relevant to securing federal information systems. These impact levels focus on the potential impact and magnitude of harm that the loss of confidentiality, integrity, or availability would have on agency operations, agency assets, or individuals. It is recognized that an information system may contain more than one type of information (e.g., privacy information, medical information, proprietary information, financial information, contractor sensitive information, system security information), each of which is subject to security categorization. The security category of an information system that processes, stores, or transmits multiple types of information should be at least the highest impact level that has been determined for each type of information for each security objective of confidentiality, integrity, and availability. The FIPS 199 security category should be considered during the risk assessment to help guide the information system owner's selection of security controls for the information system. Security categorization information is typically documented in the system identification section of the system security plan or included as an attachment to the plan.

Supplemental Guidance for Low-Impact Systems: *None.*

REFERENCES: FIPS 199; NIST Special Publications 800-18, 800-30, 800-59, 800-60, or equivalents.

THREAT IDENTIFICATION

SUBTASK 1.3: Confirm that potential threats that could exploit information system flaws or weaknesses have been identified and documented in the system security plan, risk assessment, or an equivalent document.

RESPONSIBILITY: Information System Owner.

GUIDANCE: It is important to consider all potential threats that could cause harm to an information system, ultimately affecting the confidentiality, integrity, or availability of the system. Threats can be natural (floods, earthquakes, tornadoes, landslides, avalanches, electrical storms), human (events that are either enabled by or caused by human beings), or environmental (long-term power failures, pollution, chemicals, liquid leakage). It should be noted that all possible threats that might be encountered in the environment need not be listed—only those that are relevant to the security of the information system. Threat information (including capabilities, intentions, and resources of potential adversaries) for a specific information system is generally nonspecific or incomplete at best. Recognizing the highly networked nature of the current federal computing environment, there exists an acknowledged set of baseline threats to all information systems. In other words, in today's interconnected and interdependent information systems environment, which encompasses many common platforms and technologies, there is a high likelihood of a variety of threats (both intentional and unintentional) acting to compromise the security of agency information systems. In addition to this generalized assumption about threats, specific threat information, if available, should be used during the risk assessment to help guide the selection of security controls for the information system. Threat information should be coordinated with the senior agency information security officer and authorizing official to facilitate reuse and sharing with other information system owners, agency-wide. The level of effort (i.e., degree of rigor and formality) applied to the threat identification process should be commensurate with the FIPS 199 security category of the information system (i.e., the level of effort increases as the potential impact on agency operations, agency assets, or individuals increases). Threat identification information is typically documented in the risk assessment, which should be included in the system security plan either by reference or as an attachment.

Supplemental Guidance for Low-Impact Systems: *None.*

REFERENCES: NIST Special Publications 800-18, 800-30, or equivalents.

VULNERABILITY IDENTIFICATION

SUBTASK 1.4: Confirm that flaws or weaknesses in the information system that could be exploited by potential threat sources have been identified and documented in the system security plan, risk assessment, or an equivalent document.

RESPONSIBILITY: Information System Owner.

GUIDANCE: Flaws or weaknesses in an information system that could be exploited by potential threats determine the potential vulnerabilities in that system. Vulnerability identification can be conducted at any phase in the system development life cycle. If the system is under development, the search for vulnerabilities focuses on the organization's security policies, planned security procedures, system requirement definitions, and developer security product analyses. If the system is being implemented, the identification of vulnerabilities is expanded to include more specific information, such as the planned security features described in the security design documentation and the results of the developmental security test and evaluation. If the system is operational, the process of identifying vulnerabilities includes an analysis of the system security controls employed to protect the system. The identification of vulnerabilities can be accomplished in a variety of ways using questionnaires, on-site interviews, document reviews, and automated scanning tools. Vulnerability sources include, for example: (i) previous risk assessment documentation; (ii) audit reports; (iii) system anomaly reports; (iv) security reviews; (v) self assessments; (vi) results of vulnerability scans and penetration tests; (vii) security test and evaluation reports; (viii) previous assessment reports from security certifications; (ix) vulnerability lists; (x) security advisories; (xi) vendor advisories; (xii) commercial computer incident/emergency response teams and post lists; (xiii) information security vulnerability alerts and bulletins; and (xiv) hardware, software, or firmware security analyses. Vulnerability information associated with system-specific and common security controls should be coordinated with the senior agency information security officer and authorizing officials to facilitate reuse and sharing with other information system owners agency-wide. The level of effort (i.e., degree of rigor and formality) applied to the vulnerability identification process should be commensurate with the FIPS 199 security category of the information system (i.e., the level of effort increases as the potential impact on agency operations, agency assets, or individuals increases). Vulnerability identification information is typically documented in the risk assessment report, which should be included in the system security plan either by reference or as an attachment.

Supplemental Guidance for Low-Impact Systems: *None.*

REFERENCES: NIST Special Publications 800-18, 800-30, or equivalents.

SECURITY CONTROL IDENTIFICATION

SUBTASK 1.5:   Confirm that the security controls (either planned or implemented) for the information system have been identified and documented in the system security plan or an equivalent document.

RESPONSIBILITY: Information System Owner.

GUIDANCE: Security controls for information systems are listed in NIST Special Publication 800-53, *Recommended Security Controls for Federal Information Systems*. These predefined sets of security controls (targeted to the security categories defined in FIPS 199) provide a baseline or starting point for agencies in addressing the necessary safeguards and countermeasures required for their information systems. Common security controls should be identified during a collaborative agency-wide process with the involvement of the senior agency information security officer, authorizing officials, information system owners, and information system security officers (or by the developmental program manager in the case of common security controls for common hardware software and/or firmware). Agencies should perform additional analyses to determine if adjustments to the baseline set of security controls are needed. These adjustments to the baseline set of security controls should be based on specific threat and vulnerability information generated during the risk assessment for the information system and the agency's determination of acceptable risk. Adjustments to the baseline set of security controls should be reasonable, appropriate, and fully documented in the system security plan with supporting rationale. Upon completion of the security control identification process, the agreed-upon set of controls should adequately protect the confidentiality, integrity, and availability of the system and its information. The level of effort (i.e., degree of rigor and formality) applied to the security control selection process should be commensurate with the FIPS 199 security category of the information system (i.e., the level of effort increases as the potential impact on agency operations, agency assets, or individuals increases). Security controls are typically documented in the system security plan.

Supplemental Guidance for Low-Impact Systems: *None.*

REFERENCES: NIST Special Publications 800-18, 800-30, 800-53, or equivalents.

INITIAL RISK DETERMINATION

SUBTASK 1.6:   Confirm that the risk to agency operations, agency assets, or individuals has been determined and documented in the system security plan, risk assessment, or an equivalent document.

RESPONSIBILITY: Information System Owner.

GUIDANCE: FISMA and OMB Circular A-130, Appendix III, require risk assessments as part of a risk-based approach to determining adequate, cost-effective security for an information system. The methods used to assess risk should include consideration of the major factors in risk management including: (i) threats to and vulnerabilities in the information system; (ii) potential impact and magnitude of harm to agency operations, agency assets, or individuals that could result from the unauthorized access, use, disclosure, disruption, modification, or destruction of information and the information system; and (iii) the effectiveness of current or proposed security controls. It is impractical, in most cases, to plan for or implement security controls that address all potential vulnerabilities. Vulnerabilities resulting from the absence of security controls or the ineffectiveness of controls (i.e., controls *not* implemented correctly, *not* operating as intended, or *not* producing the desired outcome with respect to meeting system security requirements) provide the basis for determining the agency-level risk posed by the operation of the information system. The level of effort (i.e., degree of rigor and formality) applied to the risk assessment should be commensurate with the FIPS 199 security category of the information system (i.e., the level of effort increases as the potential impact on agency operations, agency assets, or individuals increases). Assessing agency-level risk should be an ongoing activity to ensure that as new threats and vulnerabilities are identified, adequate security controls are implemented. Agency-level risk is typically documented in the risk assessment, which should be included in the system security plan either by reference or as an attachment.

Supplemental Guidance for Low-Impact Systems: *None.*

REFERENCES: FISMA; OMB Circular A-130, Appendix III; NIST Special Publication 800-30, or equivalent.

TASK 2: NOTIFICATION AND RESOURCE IDENTIFICATION

The objective of the notification and resource identification task is to: (i) provide notification to all concerned agency officials as to the impending security certification and accreditation of the information system; (ii) determine the resources needed to carry out the effort; and (iii) prepare a plan of execution for the certification and accreditation activities indicating the proposed schedule and key milestones.

NOTIFICATION

SUBTASK 2.1:   Inform the senior agency information security officer, authorizing official, certification agent, user representatives, and other interested agency officials that the information system requires security certification and accreditation support.

RESPONSIBILITY: Information System Owner.

GUIDANCE: The initial notification of key agency officials is an important activity to establish the security certification and accreditation process as an integral part of the system development life cycle. The notification also serves as an early warning to help prepare potential participants for the upcoming tasks that will be necessary to plan, organize, and conduct the security certification and accreditation. In some instances, the authorizing official or senior agency information security officer provides the initial notification to the information system owner and other key agency officials. This typically occurs when a specified time period has elapsed and the information system must undergo reaccreditation in accordance with federal or agency policy.

Supplemental Guidance for Low-Impact Systems: *For low-impact systems, a simplified notification procedure is recommended. The information system owner notifies the authorizing official and senior agency information security officer that a **self-assessment** of the information system security controls is planned and provides an estimated completion date.*

REFERENCE: OMB Circular A-130, Appendix III.

PLANNING AND RESOURCES

SUBTASK 2.2:   Determine the level of effort and resources required for the security certification and accreditation of the information system (including organizations involved) and prepare a plan of execution.

RESPONSIBILITY: Authorizing Official; Senior Agency Information Security Officer; Information System Owner; Certification Agent.

GUIDANCE: The level of effort required for security certification depends on: (i) the size and complexity of the information system; (ii) the FIPS 199 security category of the system; (iii) the security controls employed to protect the system; and (iv) the specific methods and procedures used to assess the security controls in the system to determine the extent to which the controls are implemented correctly, operating as intended, and producing the desired outcome with respect to meeting the security requirements for the system. Identifying appropriate resources (e.g., supporting organizations, funding, and individuals with critical skills) needed for the security certification effort is an essential aspect of the initial preparation activities and is typically integrated within the system development life cycle and capital planning and budgeting processes. Once a certification agent is selected (or certification services procured), an execution plan for conducting the security certification and accreditation is prepared by the certification agent and approved by the information system owner, authorizing official, and senior agency information security officer. The execution plan contains specific tasks, milestones, and delivery schedule. This information can be included in a system development/change plan during the initiation phase of the system development life cycle and need not be repeated in a separate plan of execution.

Supplemental Guidance for Low-Impact Systems: *For low-impact systems, a simplified planning procedure is recommended. The information system owner estimates the level of* *effort required for a **self-assessment** of the information system security controls. The authorizing official, senior agency information security officer, and independent certification agent are **not** required to participate in the process.*

REFERENCE: OMB Circular A-130, Appendix III.

TASK 3: SYSTEM SECURITY PLAN ANALYSIS, UPDATE, AND ACCEPTANCE

The objective of the system security plan analysis, update, and acceptance task is to: (i) perform an independent review of the FIPS 199 security categorization; (ii) obtain an independent analysis of the system security plan; (iii) update the system security plan as needed based on the results of the independent analysis; and (iv) obtain acceptance of the system security plan by the authorizing official and senior agency information security officer prior to conducting an assessment of the security controls in the information system. The completion of this task concludes the Initiation Phase of the security certification and accreditation process.

SECURITY CATEGORIZATION REVIEW

SUBTASK 3.1: Review the FIPS 199 security categorization described in the system security plan to determine if the assigned impact values with respect to the potential loss of confidentiality, integrity, and availability are consistent with agency's actual mission requirements.

RESPONSIBILITY: Authorizing Official; Senior Agency Information Security Officer; Certification Agent.

GUIDANCE: FIPS 199 is used as part of an agency's risk management program to help ensure that appropriate security controls are applied to each information system and that the controls are adequately assessed to determine the extent to which the controls are implemented correctly, operating as intended, and producing the desired outcome with respect to meeting the system security requirements. The review of the security categorization ensures that the information system owner has adequately reflected the importance (including criticality and sensitivity) of the information system in supporting the operations and assets of the agency. Independent review of the security categorization by the certification agent, authorizing official, and senior agency information security officer is performed as needed to ensure appropriate categorization.

Supplemental Guidance for Low-Impact Systems: *For low-impact systems, an independent certification agent is **not** required to participate in the process.*

REFERENCES: FIPS 199; NIST Special Publication 800-60, or equivalent.

SYSTEM SECURITY PLAN ANALYSIS

SUBTASK 3.2: Analyze the system security plan to determine if the vulnerabilities in the information system and the resulting risk to agency operations, agency assets, or individuals are actually what the plan would produce, if implemented.

RESPONSIBILITY: Authorizing Official; Senior Agency Information Security Officer; Certification Agent.

GUIDANCE: The system security plan provides an overview of the information system security requirements and describes the security controls in place or planned for meeting those requirements. The independent review of the system security plan by the certification agent, authorizing official, and senior agency information security officer determines if the plan is complete and consistent with the requirements document for the information system. The certification agent, authorizing official, and senior agency information security officer also determine, at the level of analysis possible only with available planning or operational documents and information from the risk assessment, if the vulnerabilities in the information system and resulting agency-level risk appear to be correct and reasonable. Based on the results of this independent review and analysis, the certification agent, authorizing official and senior agency information security officer may recommend changes to the system security plan. Whenever possible, these changes should be reflected in the requirements document for the information system.

Supplemental Guidance for Low-Impact Systems: *For low-impact systems, a simplified review process is recommended. The authorizing official and senior agency information security officer conduct a limited review of the system security plan to determine the validity of the plan. Minimal analysis is required. An independent certification agent is **not** required to participate in the process.*

REFERENCE: NIST Special Publication 800-18, or equivalent.

SYSTEM SECURITY PLAN UPDATE

SUBTASK 3.3:   Update the system security plan based on the results of the independent analysis and recommendations of the certification agent, authorizing official, and senior agency information security officer.

RESPONSIBILITY: Information System Owner.

GUIDANCE: The information system owner reviews the changes recommended by the certification agent, authorizing official, and senior agency information security officer and consults with other agency representatives (e.g., information owner, information system security officer, or user representatives) prior to making any final modifications to the system security plan. The modifications to the system security plan may include any of the areas described in Task 1 (e.g., adjusting security controls, changing vulnerabilities, or modifying the agency-level risk).

Supplemental Guidance for Low-Impact Systems: *For low-impact systems, an independent certification agent is **not** required to participate in the process.*

REFERENCE: NIST Special Publication 800-18, or equivalent.

SYSTEM SECURITY PLAN ACCEPTANCE

SUBTASK 3.4:   Review the system security plan to determine if the risk to agency operations, agency assets, or individuals is acceptable.

RESPONSIBILITY: Authorizing Official; Senior Agency Information Security Officer.

GUIDANCE: If the agency-level risk described in the system security plan (or risk assessment) is deemed unacceptable, the authorizing official and senior agency information security officer send the plan back to the information system owner for appropriate action. If the agency-level risk described in the system security plan (or risk assessment) is deemed acceptable, the authorizing official and senior agency information security officer accept the plan. The acceptance of the system security plan and agency-level risk assessment represents an important milestone in the security certification and accreditation of the information system. The authorizing official and senior agency information security officer, by accepting the system security plan, are agreeing to the set of security controls proposed to meet the security requirements for the information system. This agency-level agreement allows the security certification and accreditation process to advance to the next phase (i.e., the actual assessment of the security controls). The acceptance of the system security plan also approves the level of effort and resources required to successfully complete the associated security certification and accreditation activities.

Supplemental Guidance for Low-Impact Systems: *For low-impact systems, a simplified review process is recommended. The authorizing official and senior agency information security officer conduct a limited review of the system security plan to determine the acceptability of agency-level risk. Minimal analysis is required.*

REFERENCE: NIST Special Publication 800-30, or equivalent.

Key Milestone:

The following questions should be answered before proceeding to the Security Certification Phase—

- **Does the FIPS 199 security category of the information system described in the system security plan appear to be correct?**

- **Have the resources required to successfully complete the security certification and accreditation of the information system been identified and allocated?**

- **Does the risk to agency operations (including mission, functions, image, or reputation), agency assets, or individuals described in the system security plan appear to be correct?**

- **Having decided that the agency-level risk appears to be correct, would this risk be acceptable?**

3.2 SECURITY CERTIFICATION PHASE

The Security Certification Phase consists of two tasks: (i) security control assessment; and (ii) security certification documentation. The purpose of this phase is to determine the extent to which the security controls in the information system are implemented correctly, operating as intended, and producing the desired outcome with respect to meeting the security requirements for the system. This phase also addresses specific actions taken or planned to correct deficiencies in the security controls and to reduce or eliminate known vulnerabilities in the information system. Upon successful completion of this phase, the authorizing official will have the information needed from the security certification to determine the risk to agency operations, agency assets, or individuals—and thus will be able to render an appropriate security accreditation decision for the information system.

TASK 4: SECURITY CONTROL ASSESSMENT

The objective of the security control assessment task is to: (i) prepare for the assessment of the security controls in the information system; (ii) conduct the assessment of the security controls; and (iii) document the results of the assessment. Preparation for security assessment involves gathering appropriate planning and supporting materials, system requirements and design documentation, security control implementation evidence, and results from previous security assessments, security reviews, or audits. Preparation also involves developing specific methods and procedures to assess the security controls in the information system. The certification agent,[40] at the completion of this task, will be able to determine the extent to which the security controls

---

[40] The information system owner may assume the role of the independent certification agent when a self-assessment of the information system security controls is appropriate. The information system owner may also seek the assistance of other designated individuals (including contractors) in carrying out self-assessment activities.

in the information system are implemented correctly, operating as intended, and producing the desired outcome with respect to meeting the security requirements for the information system. The certification agent will also be in a position to make recommendations on corrective actions for security control deficiencies and offer advice to the information system owner and authorizing official on how the known vulnerabilities in the system translate into agency-level risk.

DOCUMENTATION AND SUPPORTING MATERIALS

SUBTASK 4.1:   Assemble any documentation and supporting materials necessary for the assessment of the security controls in the information system; if these documents include previous assessments of security controls, review the findings, results, and evidence.

RESPONSIBILITY: Information System Owner; Certification Agent.

GUIDANCE: The information system owner should assist the certification agent in gathering all relevant documents and supporting materials from the agency that will be required during the assessment of the security controls. Descriptive information about the information system is typically documented in the system identification section of the system security plan or in some cases, included by reference or as attachments to the plan. Supporting materials such as procedures, reports, logs, and records showing evidence of security control implementation should be identified as well. Assessing the security controls in an information system can be a very costly and time-consuming process. In order to make the security certification and accreditation process as timely and cost-effective as possible, the reuse of previous evaluation results, when reasonable and appropriate, is strongly recommended. For example, a recent audit of an information system may have produced important information about the effectiveness of selected security controls. Another opportunity, as appropriate, to reuse previous assessment results comes from programs that test and evaluate the security features of commercial information technology products. And finally, if prior assessment results from the system developer are available, the certification agent, under appropriate circumstances may incorporate those results into the security certification. Certification agents should maximize the use of previous assessment results in determining the extent to which the security controls are implemented correctly, operating as intended, and producing the desired outcome with respect to meeting the security requirements for the system.

Supplemental Guidance for Low-Impact Systems: *For low-impact systems, the information system owner may employ the services of the information system security officer or other designated individuals (including contractors) to assist in: (i) the assembly of documentation and supporting materials necessary for a **self-assessment** of the information system security controls; and (ii) the review of findings, results, and evidence from previous assessments of the security controls. An independent certification agent is **not** required to participate in the process.*

REFERENCES: Documents and supporting materials included or referenced in the system security plan; NIST Special Publication 800-53A, or equivalent; audits; security certifications; security reviews; self-assessments; security test and evaluation reports; privacy impact assessments; ISO/IEC 15408 (Common Criteria) validations; FIPS 140-2 validations.

METHODS AND PROCEDURES

SUBTASK 4.2:   Select, or develop when needed, appropriate methods and procedures to assess the management, operational, and technical security controls in the information system.

RESPONSIBILITY: Certification Agent.

GUIDANCE: In lieu of developing unique or specialized methods and procedures to assess the security controls in the information system, certification agents should consult NIST Special Publication 800-53A, which provides standardized methods and procedures for assessing the security controls listed in NIST Special Publication 800-53. The certification agent, if so directed by the information system owner, authorizing official, or senior agency information security officer, can supplement these assessment methods and procedures. Assessment methods and procedures may need to be created for those security controls employed by the agency that are not contained in NIST Special Publication 800-53. Additionally, assessment methods and procedures may need to be tailored for specific system implementations.

Supplemental Guidance for Low-Impact Systems: *For low-impact systems, the information system owner may employ the services of the information system security officer or other designated individuals (including contractors) to select or develop when needed, the appropriate methods and procedures necessary to conduct a **self-assessment** of the information system security controls. An independent certification agent is **not** required to participate in the process.*

REFERENCE: NIST Special Publication 800-53A, or equivalent.

SECURITY ASSESSMENT

SUBTASK 4.3:   Assess the management, operational, and technical security controls in the information system using methods and procedures selected or developed.

RESPONSIBILITY: Certification Agent.

GUIDANCE: Security assessment determines the extent to which the security controls are implemented correctly, operating as intended, and producing the desired outcome with respect to meeting the security requirements for the system. The results of the security assessment, including recommendations for correcting any deficiencies in the security controls, are documented in the security assessment report.

Supplemental Guidance for Low-Impact Systems: *For low-impact systems, the information system owner may employ the services of the information system security officer or other designated individuals (including contractors) to conduct a **self-assessment** of the information system security controls. An independent certification agent is **not** required to participate in the process.*

REFERENCE: NIST Special Publication 800-53A, or equivalent.

SECURITY ASSESSMENT REPORT

SUBTASK 4.4:   Prepare the final security assessment report.

RESPONSIBILITY: Certification Agent.

GUIDANCE: The security assessment report contains: (i) the results of the security assessment (i.e., the determination of the extent to which the security controls are implemented correctly, operating as intended, and producing the desired outcome with respect to meeting the security requirements for the system); and (ii) recommendations for correcting deficiencies in the security controls and reducing or eliminating identified vulnerabilities. The security assessment report is part of the final accreditation package along with the updated system security plan and plan of action and milestones. The security assessment report is the certification agent's statement regarding the security status of the information system.

Supplemental Guidance for Low-Impact Systems: *For low-impact systems, the information system owner may employ the services of the information system security officer or other designated individuals (including contractors) to prepare the security assessment report containing the results of the **self-assessment** of the information system security controls. The security assessment report can be a short and concise document synopsizing the **self-assessment** results and highlighting those areas that need further attention. An independent certification agent is **not** required to participate in the process.*

REFERENCE: NIST Special Publication 800-53A, or equivalent.

TASK 5: SECURITY CERTIFICATION DOCUMENTATION

The objective of the security certification documentation task is to: (i) provide the certification findings and recommendations to the information system owner; (ii) update the system security plan as needed; (iii) prepare the plan of action and milestones; and (iv) assemble the accreditation package. The information system owner has an opportunity to reduce or eliminate vulnerabilities in the information system prior to the assembly and compilation of the accreditation package and submission to the authorizing official. This is accomplished by implementing corrective actions recommended by the certification agent. The certification agent should assess any security controls modified, enhanced, or added during this process. The completion of this task concludes the Security Certification Phase.

FINDINGS AND RECOMMENDATIONS

SUBTASK 5.1:   Provide the information system owner with the security assessment report.

RESPONSIBILITY: Certification Agent.

GUIDANCE: The information system owner relies on the security expertise and the technical judgment of the certification agent to: (i) assess the security controls in the information system; and (ii) provide specific recommendations on how to correct deficiencies in the controls and reduce or eliminate identified vulnerabilities. The information system owner may choose to act on selected recommendations of the certification agent before the accreditation package is finalized if there are specific opportunities to correct deficiencies in security controls and reduce or eliminate vulnerabilities in the information system. To ensure effective allocation of resources agency-wide, any actions taken by the information system owner prior to the final accreditation decision should be coordinated with the authorizing official and senior agency information security officer. The certification agent assesses any changes made to the security controls in response to corrective actions by the information system owner and updates the assessment report, as appropriate.

Supplemental Guidance for Low-Impact Systems: *For low-impact systems, the information system security officer or other designated individuals (including contractors) provide the information system owner with the security assessment report containing the summarized results of the **self-assessment** of the information system security controls. An independent certification agent is **not** required to participate in the process.*

REFERENCE: NIST Special Publication 800-30, or equivalent.

SYSTEM SECURITY PLAN UPDATE

SUBTASK 5.2:   Update the system security plan (and risk assessment) based on the results of the security assessment and any modifications to the security controls in the information system.

RESPONSIBILITY: Information System Owner.

GUIDANCE: The system security plan should reflect the actual state of the security controls after the security assessment and any modifications by the information system owner in addressing the recommendations for corrective actions from the certification agent. At the completion of the Security Certification Phase, the security plan and risk assessment should contain an accurate list and description of the security controls implemented and a list of identified vulnerabilities (i.e., controls not implemented).

Supplemental Guidance for Low-Impact Systems: *For low-impact systems, an independent certification agent is **not** required to participate in the process.*

REFERENCE: NIST Special Publication 800-18, or equivalent.

PLAN OF ACTION AND MILESTONES PREPARATION

SUBTASK 5.3: Prepare the plan of action and milestones based on the results of the security assessment.

RESPONSIBILITY: Information System Owner.

GUIDANCE: The plan of action and milestones document, one of the three key documents in the security accreditation package, describes actions taken or planned by the information system owner to correct deficiencies in the security controls and to address remaining vulnerabilities in the information system (i.e., reduce, eliminate, or accept the vulnerabilities). The plan of actions and milestones document identifies: (i) the tasks needing to be accomplished; (ii) the resources required to accomplish the elements of the plan; (iii) any milestones in meeting the tasks; and (iv) scheduled completion dates for the milestones.

Supplemental Guidance for Low-Impact Systems: *None.*

REFERENCE: OMB Memorandum 02-01.

ACCREDITATION PACKAGE ASSEMBLY

SUBTASK 5.4: Assemble the final security accreditation package and submit to authorizing official.

RESPONSIBILITY: Information System Owner.

GUIDANCE: The information system owner is responsible for the assembly and compilation of the final security accreditation package with inputs from the information system security officer and the certification agent. The accreditation package contains: (i) the security assessment report from the certification agent providing the results of the independent assessment of the security controls and recommendations for corrective actions; (ii) the plan of action and milestones from the information system owner indicating actions taken or planned to correct deficiencies in the controls and to reduce or eliminate vulnerabilities in the information system; and (iii) the updated system security plan with the latest copy of the risk assessment. Certification agent input to the final accreditation package provides an unbiased and independent view of the extent to which the security controls in the information system are implemented correctly, operating as intended, and producing the desired outcome with respect to meeting the system security requirements. The information system owner may also wish to consult with other key agency participants (e.g., the user representatives) prior to submitting the final accreditation package to the authorizing official. The authorizing official will use this information during the Security Accreditation Phase to determine the risk to agency operations, agency assets, or individuals. The accreditation package can be submitted in either paper or electronic form. The contents of the accreditation package should be protected appropriately in accordance with agency policy.

Supplemental Guidance for Low-Impact Systems: *For low-impact systems, the security accreditation package consists of: (i) the updated system security plan; (ii) an abbreviated security assessment report (i.e., a brief summary of the self-assessment results); and (iii) a plan of action and milestones.*

REFERENCE: OMB Circular A-130, Appendix III.

Key Milestone:

The following questions should be answered before proceeding to the Security Accreditation Phase—

- **To what extent are the security controls in the information system implemented correctly, operating as intended, and producing the desired outcome with respect to meeting the security requirements for the system?**

- **What specific actions have been taken or are planned to correct deficiencies in the security controls and to reduce or eliminate known vulnerabilities in the information system?**

3.3 SECURITY ACCREDITATION PHASE

The Security Accreditation Phase consists of two tasks: (i) security accreditation decision; and (ii) security accreditation documentation. The purpose of this phase is to determine if the remaining known vulnerabilities in the information system (after the implementation of an agreed-upon set of security controls) pose an acceptable level of risk to agency operations, agency assets, or individuals. Upon successful completion of this phase, the information system owner will have: (i) authorization to operate the information system; (ii) an interim authorization to operate the information system under specific terms and conditions; or (iii) denial of authorization to operate the information system.

TASK 6: SECURITY ACCREDITATION DECISION

The objective of the security accreditation decision task is to: (i) determine the risk to agency operations, agency assets, or individuals; and (ii) determine if the agency-level risk is acceptable. The authorizing official, working with information from the information system owner, information system security officer, and certification agent produced during the previous phase, has independent confirmation of the identified vulnerabilities in the information system and a list of planned or completed corrective actions to reduce or eliminate those vulnerabilities. It is this information that is used to determine the final risk to the agency and the acceptability of that risk.

FINAL RISK DETERMINATION

SUBTASK 6.1:   Determine the risk to agency operations, agency assets, or individuals based on the vulnerabilities in the information system and any planned or completed corrective actions to reduce or eliminate those vulnerabilities.

RESPONSIBILITY: Authorizing Official.

GUIDANCE: The authorizing official receives the final security accreditation package from the information system owner. The vulnerabilities in the information system confirmed by the certification agent should be assessed to determine how those particular vulnerabilities translate into risk to agency operations, agency assets, or individuals. The authorizing official or designated representative should judge which information system vulnerabilities are of greatest concern to the agency and which vulnerabilities can be tolerated without creating unreasonable agency-level risk. The plan of action and milestones (i.e., actions taken or planned to correct deficiencies in the security controls and reduce or eliminate vulnerabilities) submitted by the information system owner should also be considered in determining the risk to the agency. The authorizing official may consult the information system owner, certification agent, or other agency officials before making the final risk determination.

Supplemental Guidance for Low-Impact Systems: *For low-impact systems, a simplified process for risk determination is recommended. The level of effort by the authorizing official in determining risk should be minimal since the potential impact on agency operations, agency assets, and/or individuals has already been determined to be low. An independent certification agent is **not** required to participate in the process.*

REFERENCE: NIST Special Publication 800-30, or equivalent.

RISK ACCEPTABILITY

SUBTASK 6.2:   Determine if the risk to agency operations, agency assets, or individuals is acceptable and prepare the final security accreditation decision letter.

RESPONSIBILITY: Authorizing Official.

GUIDANCE: The authorizing official should consider many factors when deciding if the risk to agency operations, agency assets, or individuals is acceptable. Balancing security considerations with mission and operational needs is paramount to achieving an acceptable accreditation decision. The authorizing official renders an accreditation decision for the information system after reviewing all of the relevant information and, where appropriate, consulting with key agency officials.

If, after assessing the results of the security certification, the authorizing official deems that the agency-level risk is acceptable, an authorization to operate is issued. The information system is accredited without any restrictions or limitations on its operation.

If, after assessing the results of the security certification, the authorizing official deems that the agency-level risk is unacceptable, but there is an important mission-related need to place the information system into operation, an interim authorization to operate may be issued. The interim authorization to operate is a limited authorization under specific terms and conditions including corrective actions to be taken by the information system owner and a required timeframe for completion of those actions. A detailed plan of action and milestones should be submitted by the information system owner and approved by the authorizing official prior to the interim authorization to operate taking effect. The information system is *not* accredited during the period of limited authorization to operate. The information system owner is responsible for completing the corrective actions identified in the plan of action and milestones and resubmitting an updated security accreditation package upon completion of those actions.

If, after assessing the results of the security certification, the authorizing official deems that the agency-level risk is unacceptable, the information system is not authorized for operation and thus is *not* accredited.

The authorizing official's designated representative or administrative staff prepares the final security accreditation decision letter. The letter includes the accreditation decision, the rationale for the decision, the terms and conditions for information system operation, and required corrective actions, if appropriate. The accreditation decision letter indicates to the information system owner whether the system is: (i) authorized to operate; (ii) authorized to operate on an interim basis under strict terms and conditions; or (iii) not authorized to operate. The supporting rationale provides the information system owner with the justification for the authorizing official's decision. The terms and conditions for the authorization provide a description of any limitations or restrictions placed on the operation of the information system that must be adhered to by the information system owner. The security accreditation letter is included in the final accreditation package. The contents of the accreditation package should be protected appropriately in accordance with agency policy.

Supplemental Guidance for Low-Impact Systems: *For low-impact systems, a simplified process for the determination of risk acceptability is recommended. The level of effort by the authorizing official in determining risk acceptability should be minimal since the potential impact on agency operations, agency assets, and/or individuals has already been determined to be low.*

REFERENCE: OMB Circular A-130, Appendix III.

TASK 7: SECURITY ACCREDITATION DOCUMENTATION

The objective of the security accreditation documentation task is to: (i) transmit the final security accreditation package to the appropriate individuals and organizations; and (ii) update the system security plan with the latest information from the accreditation decision. The completion of this task concludes the Security Accreditation Phase of the security certification and accreditation process.

SECURITY ACCREDITATION PACKAGE TRANSMISSION

SUBTASK 7.1:   Provide copies of the final security accreditation package including the accreditation decision letter (in either paper or electronic form), to the information system owner and any other agency officials having an interest (i.e., need to know) in the security of the information system.

RESPONSIBILITY: Authorizing Official.

GUIDANCE: The security accreditation package including the accreditation decision letter is returned to the information system owner. Upon receipt of the security accreditation decision letter and accreditation package, the information system owner accepts the terms and conditions of the authorization. The original accreditation package is kept on file by the information system owner. The authorizing official and senior agency information security officer also retain copies of the decision letter and accreditation package. The accreditation package contains important documents and as such, should be appropriately safeguarded and stored, whenever possible, in a centralized agency filing system to ensure accessibility. The accreditation package should also be readily available to auditors and oversight agencies upon request. The accreditation package including all supporting documents, should be retained in accordance with the agency's records retention policy.

Supplemental Guidance for Low-Impact Systems: *None.*

REFERENCE: OMB Circular A-130, Appendix III.

SYSTEM SECURITY PLAN UPDATE

SUBTASK 7.2:   Update the system security plan based on the final determination of risk to agency operations, agency assets, or individuals.

RESPONSIBILITY: Information System Owner.

GUIDANCE: The system security plan should be updated to reflect any changes in the information system resulting from the Security Accreditation Phase. Any conditions set forth in the accreditation decision should also be noted in the plan. It is expected that the changes to the system security plan at this phase in the security certification and accreditation process would be minimal.

Supplemental Guidance for Low-Impact Systems: *None.*

REFERENCE: NIST Special Publication 800-18, or equivalent.

Key Milestone:

The following questions should be answered before proceeding to the Continuous Monitoring Phase—

– **How do the known vulnerabilities in the information system translate into agency-level risk— that is, risk to agency operations, agency assets, or individuals?**

– **Is this agency-level risk acceptable?**

3.4 CONTINOUS MONITORING PHASE

The Continuous Monitoring Phase consists of three tasks: (i) configuration management and control; (ii) security control monitoring; and (iii) status reporting and documentation. The purpose of this phase is to provide oversight and monitoring of the security controls in the information system on an ongoing basis and to inform the authorizing official when changes occur that may impact on the security of the system. The activities in this phase are performed continuously throughout the life cycle of the information system. Reaccreditation may be required because of specific changes to the information system or because federal or agency policies require periodic reaccreditation of the information system.

TASK 8: CONFIGURATION MANAGEMENT AND CONTROL

The objective of the configuration management and control task is to: (i) document the proposed or actual changes to the information system; and (ii) determine the impact of proposed or actual changes on the security of the system. An information system will typically be in a constant state of migration with upgrades to hardware, software, or firmware and possible modifications to the system environment. Documenting information system changes and assessing the potential impact on the security of the system on an ongoing basis is an essential aspect of maintaining the security accreditation.

DOCUMENTATION OF INFORMATION SYSTEM CHANGES

SUBTASK 8.1:   Using established agency configuration management and control procedures, document proposed or actual changes to the information system (including hardware, software, firmware, and surrounding environment).

RESPONSIBILITY: Information System Owner.

GUIDANCE: An orderly and disciplined approach to managing, controlling, and documenting changes to an information system is critical to the continuous assessment of the security controls that protect the system. It is important to record any relevant information about the specific proposed or actual changes to the hardware, firmware, or software such as version or release numbers, descriptions of new or modified features or capabilities, and security implementation guidance. It is also important to record any changes to the information system environment such as modifications to the physical plant. The information system owner and information system security officer should use this information in assessing the potential security impact of the proposed or actual changes to the information system. Significant changes to the information system should not be undertaken prior to assessing the security impact of such changes.

Supplemental Guidance for Low-Impact Systems: *None.*

REFERENCES: Agency policies/procedures on configuration management and control.

SECURITY IMPACT ANALYSIS

SUBTASK 8.2: Analyze the proposed or actual changes to the information system (including hardware, software, firmware, and surrounding environment) to determine the security impact of such changes.

RESPONSIBILITY: Information System Owner.

GUIDANCE: Changes to the information system may affect the security controls currently in place, produce new vulnerabilities in the system, or generate requirements for new security controls that were not needed previously. If the results of the security impact analysis indicate that the proposed or actual changes to the information system will affect or have affected the security of the information system, corrective actions should be initiated and the plan of action and milestones revised. The information system owner or information system security officer may wish to consult with the user representatives or other agency officials prior to implementing any security-related changes to the information system. Conducting a security impact analysis is part of the ongoing assessment of risk within the agency. The level of effort (i.e., degree of rigor and formality) applied to the security impact analysis should be commensurate with the FIPS 199 security category of the information system (i.e., the level of effort increases as the potential impact on agency operations, agency assets, or individuals increases).

Supplemental Guidance for Low-Impact Systems: *None.*

REFERENCE: NIST Special Publication 800-30, or equivalent.

TASK 9: SECURITY CONTROL MONITORING

The objective of the security control monitoring task is to: (i) select an appropriate set of security controls in the information system to be monitored; and (ii) assess the designated controls using methods and procedures selected by the information system owner. The continuous monitoring of security controls helps to identify potential security-related problems in the information system that are not identified during the security impact analysis conducted as part of the configuration management and control process.

SECURITY CONTROL SELECTION

SUBTASK 9.1: Select the security controls in the information system to be monitored on a continuous basis.

RESPONSIBILITY: Information System Owner.

GUIDANCE: The criteria established by the information system owner for selecting which security controls will be monitored should reflect the agency's priorities and importance of the information system to the agency. For example, certain security controls may be considered more critical than other controls because of the potential impact on the information system if those controls were subverted or found to be ineffective. The security controls being monitored should be reviewed over time to ensure that a representative sample of controls is included in the ongoing security assessments. The authorizing official and information system owner should agree on the subset of security controls in the information system that should be monitored as well as the frequency of such monitoring activity. The level of effort (i.e., degree of rigor and formality) applied to the security control selection process should be commensurate with the FIPS 199 security category of the information system (i.e., the level of effort increases as the potential impact on agency operations, agency assets, or individuals increases).

Supplemental Guidance for Low-Impact Systems: *None.*

REFERENCES: FISMA; OMB Circular A-130, Appendix III; NIST Special Publication 800-53.

SELECTED SECURITY CONTROL ASSESSMENT

SUBTASK 9.2:   Assess an agreed-upon set of security controls in the information system to determine the extent to which the controls are implemented correctly, operating as intended, and producing the desired outcome with respect to meeting the security requirements for the system.

RESPONSIBILITY: Information System Owner.

GUIDANCE: The continuous monitoring of security controls can be accomplished in a variety of ways including security reviews, self-assessments, security testing and evaluation, or audits. The methods and procedures employed to assess the security controls during the monitoring process are at the discretion of the information system owner. In lieu of developing unique or specialized methods and procedures to assess the security controls in the information system, information system owners should consult NIST Special Publication 800-53A, which provides standardized assessment methods and procedures for the security controls listed in NIST Special Publication 800-53. The monitoring process should be documented and available for review by the authorizing official or senior agency information security officer, upon request. If the results of the security assessment indicate that selected controls are less than effective in their application and are affecting the security of the information system, corrective actions should be initiated and the plan of action and milestones updated. The level of effort (i.e., degree of rigor and formality) applied to the assessment of security controls should be commensurate with the FIPS 199 security category of the information system (i.e., the level of effort increases as the potential impact on agency operations, agency assets, or individuals increases).

Supplemental Guidance for Low-Impact Systems: *None.*

REFERENCES: FISMA; OMB Circular A-130, Appendix III; NIST Special Publication 800-53A.

TASK 10: STATUS REPORTING AND DOCUMENTATION

The objective of the status reporting and documentation task is to: (i) update the system security plan to reflect the proposed or actual changes to the information system; (ii) update the plan of action and milestones based on the activities carried out during the continuous monitoring phase; and (iii) report the security status of the information system to the authorizing official and senior agency information security officer. The information in the security status reports (typically conveyed through updated plans of action and milestones) should be used to determine the need for security reaccreditation and to satisfy FISMA reporting requirements.

SYSTEM SECURITY PLAN UPDATE

SUBTASK 10.1:   Update the system security plan based on the documented changes to the information system (including hardware, software, firmware, and surrounding environment) and the results of the continuous monitoring process.

RESPONSIBILITY: Information System Owner.

GUIDANCE: The system security plan should contain the most up-to-date information about the information system. Changes to the information system should be reflected in the system security plan. The frequency of system security plan updates is at the discretion of the information system owner. The updates should occur at appropriate intervals to capture significant changes to the information system, but not so frequently as to generate unnecessary paperwork. The Chief Information Officer, senior agency information security officer, authorizing official, information system owner, information system security officer, and certification agent will be using the system security plan to guide any future security certification and accreditation activities, when required.

Supplemental Guidance for Low-Impact Systems: *None.*

REFERENCE: NIST Special Publication 800-18, or equivalent.

PLAN OF ACTION AND MILESTONES UPDATE

SUBTASK 10.2:   Update the plan of action and milestones based on the documented changes to the information system (including hardware, software, firmware, and surrounding environment) and the results of the continuous monitoring process.

RESPONSIBILITY: Information System Owner.

GUIDANCE: The plan of action and milestones is used by the authorizing official to monitor the progress in correcting deficiencies noted during the security certification. The plan of action and milestones should: (i) report progress made on the current outstanding items listed in the plan; (ii) address vulnerabilities in the information system discovered during the security impact analysis or security control monitoring; and (iii) describe how the information system owner intends to address those vulnerabilities (i.e., reduce, eliminate, or accept the identified vulnerabilities). The frequency of the plan of action and milestones updates is at the discretion of the information system owner. The updates should occur at appropriate intervals to capture significant changes to the information system, but not so frequently as to generate unnecessary paperwork. The Chief Information Officer, senior agency information security officer, authorizing official, information system owner, information system security officer, and certification agent will be using the plan of action and milestones to guide any future security certification and accreditation activities, when required.

Supplemental Guidance for Low-Impact Systems: *None.*

REFERENCE: OMB Memorandum 02-01.

SUBTASK 10.3:   Report the security status of the information system to the authorizing official and senior agency information security officer.

RESPONSIBILITY: Information System Owner.

GUIDANCE: The security status report (which can be submitted in the form of an updated plan of action and milestones) should describe the continuous monitoring activities employed by the information system owner. The security status report addresses vulnerabilities in the information system discovered during the security certification, security impact analysis, and security control monitoring and how the information system owner intends to address those vulnerabilities (i.e., reduce, eliminate, or accept the vulnerabilities). The frequency of security status reports is at the discretion of the agency. The status reports should occur at appropriate intervals to transmit significant security-related information about the system, but not so frequently as to generate unnecessary paperwork. The authorizing official and the senior agency information system security officer should use the security status reports to determine if a security reaccreditation is necessary. The authorizing official should notify the information system owner if there is a decision to require a reaccreditation of the information system. A decision to reaccredit the information system should begin, as in the original security accreditation, with the Initiation Phase. The security status report should be marked and handled in accordance with agency policy. At the discretion of the agency, the security status reports on agency information systems can be used to help satisfy the FISMA reporting requirement for documenting remedial actions for any security-related deficiencies.

Supplemental Guidance for Low-Impact Systems: *None.*

REFERENCES: FISMA; OMB Circular A-130, Appendix III.

Key Milestone:

The following questions should be answered before reinitiating the certification and accreditation process—

-   **Have any changes to the information system affected the security controls in the system or introduced new vulnerabilities into the system?**

-   **If so, has the agency-level risk—that is, the risk to agency operations, agency assets, or individuals been affected? or**

-   **Has a specified time period passed requiring the information system to be reauthorized in accordance with federal or agency policy?**

APPENDIX A

REFERENCES

LAWS, DIRECTIVES, POLICIES, STANDARDS, AND GUIDELINES

1. Privacy Act of 1974 (Public Law 93-579), September 1975.

2. Paperwork Reduction Act of 1995 (Public Law 104-13), May 1995.

3. Information Technology Management Reform Act of 1996 (Public Law 104-106), August 1996.

4. Federal Information Security Management Act of 2002 (Public Law 107-347), December 2002.

5. OMB Circular A-130, Appendix III, Transmittal Memorandum #4, *Management of Federal Information Resources*, November 2000.

6. Federal Information Processing Standards (FIPS) 199, *Standards for Security Categorization of Federal Information and Information Systems*, December 2003.

7. Federal Information Processing Standards (FIPS) 200, *Security Controls for Federal Information Systems* (projected for publication December 2005).

8. Committee for National Security Systems Instruction 4009, *National Information Assurance Glossary*, revised May 2003.

9. NIST Special Publication 800-18, *Guide for Developing Security Plans for Information Technology Systems*, December 1998.

10. NIST Special Publication 800-26, *Security Self-Assessment Guide for Information Technology Systems*, November 2001.

11. NIST Special Publication 800-30, *Risk Management Guide for Information Technology Systems*, January 2002.

12. NIST Special Publication 800-34, *Contingency Planning Guide for Information Technology Systems*, June 2002.

13. NIST Special Publication 800-47, *Security Guide for Interconnecting Information Technology Systems*, September 2002.

14. NIST Special Publication 800-59, *Guideline for Identifying an Information System as a National Security System*, August 2003.

15. NIST Special Publication 800-50, *Building an Information Technology Security Awareness and Training Program*, October 2003.

16. NIST Special Publication 800-64, *Security Considerations in the Information System Development Life Cycle*, October 2003.

17. NIST Special Publication 800-53, *Recommended Security Controls for Federal Information Systems* (Initial public draft), October 2003.

18. NIST Special Publication 800-60, *Guide for Mapping Information and Information Types to Security Objectives and Risk Levels* (Second public draft), March 2004.

19. NIST Special Publication 800-61, *Computer Security Incident Handling Guide*, January 2004.

20. NIST Special Publication 800-53A, *Guide for Assessing the Security Controls in Federal Information Systems* (Initial public draft), Summer 2004.

APPENDIX B

GLOSSARY

COMMON TERMS AND DEFINITIONS

Accreditation	The official management decision given by a senior agency official to authorize operation of an information system and to explicitly accept the risk to agency operations (including mission, functions, image, or reputation), agency assets, or individuals, based on the implementation of an agreed-upon set of security controls.
Accreditation Boundary	All components of an information system to be accredited by an authorizing official and excludes separately accredited systems, to which the information system is connected. Synonymous with the term *security perimeter* defined in CNSS Instruction 4009 and DCID 6/3.
Accreditation Package	The evidence provided to the authorizing official to be used in the security accreditation decision process. Evidence includes, but is not limited to: (i) the system security plan; (ii) the assessment results from the security certification; and (iii) the plan of action and milestones.
Accrediting Authority	See Authorizing Official.
Adequate Security [OMB Circular A-130, Appendix III]	Security commensurate with the risk and the magnitude of harm resulting from the loss, misuse, or unauthorized access to or modification of information.
Agency	See Executive Agency.
Application [OMB Circular A-130, Appendix III]	The use of information resources (information and information technology) to satisfy a specific set of user requirements.
Assessment Method	A focused activity or action employed by an assessor for evaluating a particular attribute of a security control.
Assessment Procedure	A set of activities or actions employed by an assessor to determine the extent to which a security control is implemented correctly, operating as intended, and producing the desired outcome with respect to meeting the security requirements for the system.
Authenticity	The property of being genuine and being able to be verified and trusted; confidence in the validity of a transmission, a message, or message originator. See authentication.

Authentication	Verifying the identity of a user, process, or device, often as a prerequisite to allowing access to resources in an information system.
Authorization	See Accreditation.
Authorize Processing	See Accreditation.
Authorizing Official	Official with the authority to formally assume responsibility for operating an information system at an acceptable level of risk to agency operations (including mission, functions, image, or reputation), agency assets, or individuals.
Authorizing Official Designated Representative	Individual selected by an authorizing official to act on their behalf in coordinating and carrying out the necessary activities required during the security certification and accreditation of an information system.
Availability [44 U.S.C., Sec. 3542]	Ensuring timely and reliable access to and use of information.
Designated Approving (Accrediting) Authority	See Authorizing Official.
Certification Agent	The individual, group, or organization responsible for conducting a security certification.
Certification	A comprehensive assessment of the management, operational, and technical security controls in an information system, made in support of security accreditation, to determine the extent to which the controls are implemented correctly, operating as intended, and producing the desired outcome with respect to meeting the security requirements for the system.
Chief Information Officer [44 U.S.C., Sec. 5125(b)]	Agency official responsible for: (i) Providing advice and other assistance to the head of the executive agency and other senior management personnel of the agency to ensure that information technology is acquired and information resources are managed in a manner that is consistent with laws, Executive Orders, directives, policies, regulations, and priorities established by the head of the agency; (ii) Developing, maintaining, and facilitating the implementation of a sound and integrated information technology architecture for the agency; and (iii) Promoting the effective and efficient design and operation of all major information resources management processes for the agency, including improvements to work processes of the agency.

Common Security Control	Security control that can be applied to one or more agency information systems and has the following properties: (i) the development, implementation, and assessment of the control can be assigned to a responsible official or organizational element (other than the information system owner); and (ii) the results from the assessment of the control can be used to support the security certification and accreditation processes of an agency information system where that control has been applied.
Confidentiality [44 U.S.C., Sec. 3542]	Preserving authorized restrictions on information access and disclosure, including means for protecting personal privacy and proprietary information.
Countermeasures [CNSS Inst. 4009]	Actions, devices, procedures, techniques, or other measures that reduce the vulnerability of an information system. Synonymous with security controls and safeguards.
Configuration Control [CNSS Inst. 4009]	Process for controlling modifications to hardware, firmware, software, and documentation to ensure the information system is protected against improper modifications prior to, during, and after system implementation.
Executive Agency [41 U.S.C., Sec. 403]	An executive department specified in 5 U.S.C., Sec. 101; a military department specified in 5 U.S.C., Sec. 102; an independent establishment as defined in 5 U.S.C., Sec. 104(1); and a wholly owned Government corporation fully subject to the provisions of 31 U.S.C., Chapter 91.
Federal Information System [40 U.S.C., Sec. 11331]	An information system used or operated by an executive agency, by a contractor of an executive agency, or by another organization on behalf of an executive agency.
General Support System [OMB Circular A-130, Appendix III]	An interconnected set of information resources under the same direct management control that shares common functionality. It normally includes hardware, software, information, data, applications, communications, and people.
Information [FIPS 199]	An instance of an information type.
Information Owner [CNSS Inst. 4009]	Official with statutory or operational authority for specified information and responsibility for establishing the controls for its generation, collection, processing, dissemination, and disposal.
Information Resources [44 U.S.C., Sec. 3502]	Information and related resources, such as personnel, equipment, funds, and information technology.
Information Security [44 U.S.C., Sec. 3542]	The protection of information and information systems from unauthorized access, use, disclosure, disruption, modification, or destruction in order to provide confidentiality, integrity, and availability.

Information Security Policy [CNSS Inst. 4009]	Aggregate of directives, regulations, rules, and practices that prescribes how an organization manages, protects, and distributes information.
Information System [44 U.S.C., Sec. 3502] [OMB Circular A-130, Appendix III]	A discrete set of information resources organized for the collection, processing, maintenance, use, sharing, dissemination, or disposition of information.
Information System Owner (or Program Manager) [CNSS Inst. 4009, Adapted]	Official responsible for the overall procurement, development, integration, modification, or operation and maintenance of an information system.
Information System Security Officer [CNSS Inst. 4009, Adapted]	Individual responsible to the senior agency information security officer, authorizing official, or information system owner for ensuring the appropriate operational security posture is maintained for an information system or program.
Information Technology [40 U.S.C., Sec. 1401]	Any equipment or interconnected system or subsystem of equipment that is used in the automatic acquisition, storage, manipulation, management, movement, control, display, switching, interchange, transmission, or reception of data or information by the executive agency. For purposes of the preceding sentence, equipment is used by an executive agency if the equipment is used by the executive agency directly or is used by a contractor under a contract with the executive agency which: (i) requires the use of such equipment; or (ii) requires the use, to a significant extent, of such equipment in the performance of a service or the furnishing of a product. The term information technology includes computers, ancillary equipment, software, firmware and similar procedures, services (including support services), and related resources.
Information Type [FIPS 199]	A specific category of information (e.g., privacy, medical, proprietary, financial, investigative, contractor sensitive, security management), defined by an organization or in some instances, by a specific law, Executive Order, directive, policy, or regulation.
Integrity [44 U.S.C., Sec. 3542]	Guarding against improper information modification or destruction, and includes ensuring information non-repudiation and authenticity.
Major Application [OMB Circular A-130, Appendix III]	An application that requires special attention to security due to the risk and magnitude of harm resulting from the loss, misuse, or unauthorized access to or modification of the information in the application.

Major Information System [FISMA]	An information system that requires special management attention because of its importance to an agency mission; its high development, operating, or maintenance costs; or its significant role in the administration of agency programs, finances, property, or other resources.
Management Controls [NIST SP 800-18]	The security controls (i.e., safeguards or countermeasures) for an information system that focus on the management of risk and the management of information system security.
Minor Application	An application, other than a major application, that requires attention to security due to the risk and magnitude of harm resulting from the loss, misuse, or unauthorized access to or modification of the information in the application. Minor applications are typically included as part of a general support system.
National Security Information	Information that has been determined pursuant to Executive Order 12958 as amended by Executive Order 13292, or any predecessor order, or by the Atomic Energy Act of 1954, as amended, to require protection against unauthorized disclosure and is marked to indicate its classified status.
National Security System [44 U.S.C., Sec. 3542]	Any information system (including any telecommunications system) used or operated by an agency or by a contractor of an agency, or other organization on behalf of an agency— (i) the function, operation, or use of which involves intelligence activities; involves cryptologic activities related to national security; involves command and control of military forces; involves equipment that is an integral part of a weapon or weapons system; or is critical to the direct fulfillment of military or intelligence missions (excluding a system that is to be used for routine administrative and business applications, for example, payroll, finance, logistics, and personnel management applications); or, (ii) is protected at all times by procedures established for information that have been specifically authorized under criteria established by an Executive Order or an Act of Congress to be kept classified in the interest of national defense or foreign policy.
Non-repudiation [CNSS Inst. 4009]	Assurance that the sender of information is provided with proof of delivery and the recipient is provided with proof of the sender's identity, so neither can later deny having processed the information.
Operational Controls [NIST SP 800-18]	The security controls (i.e., safeguards or countermeasures) for an information system that primarily are implemented and executed by people (as opposed to systems).

Plan of Action and Milestones [OMB Memorandum 02-01]	A document that identifies tasks needing to be accomplished. It details resources required to accomplish the elements of the plan, any milestones in meeting the tasks, and scheduled completion dates for the milestones.
Potential Impact [FIPS 199]	Low: The loss of confidentiality, integrity, or availability could be expected to have a *limited* adverse effect on organizational operations, organizational assets, or individuals.
	Moderate: The loss of confidentiality, integrity, or availability could be expected to have a *serious* adverse effect on organizational operations, organizational assets, or individuals.
	High: The loss of confidentiality, integrity, or availability could be expected to have a *severe* or *catastrophic* adverse effect on organizational operations, organizational assets, or individuals.
Risk [NIST SP 800-30]	The level of impact on agency operations (including mission, functions, image, or reputation), agency assets, or individuals resulting from the operation of an information system given the potential impact of a threat and the likelihood of that threat occurring.
Risk Assessment [NIST SP 800-30]	The process of identifying risks to agency operations (including mission, functions, image, or reputation), agency assets, or individuals by determining the probability of occurrence, the resulting impact, and additional security controls that would mitigate this impact. Part of risk management, synonymous with risk analysis, and incorporates threat and vulnerability analyses.
Risk Management [NIST SP 800-30]	The process of managing risks to agency operations (including mission, functions, image, or reputation), agency assets, or individuals resulting from the operation of an information system. It includes risk assessment; cost-benefit analysis; the selection, implementation, and assessment of security controls; and the formal authorization to operate the system. The process considers effectiveness, efficiency, and constraints due to laws, directives, policies, or regulations.
Safeguards [CNSS Inst. 4009, Adapted]	Protective measures prescribed to meet the security requirements (i.e., confidentiality, integrity, and availability) specified for an information system. Safeguards may include security features, management constraints, personnel security, and security of physical structures, areas, and devices. Synonymous with security controls and countermeasures.
Security Authorization	See Accreditation.
Security Accreditation	See Accreditation.

Security Category [FIPS 199]	The characterization of information or an information system based on an assessment of the potential impact that a loss of confidentiality, integrity, or availability of such information or information system would have on organizational operations, organizational assets, or individuals.
Security Controls [FIPS 199]	The management, operational, and technical controls (i.e., safeguards or countermeasures) prescribed for an information system to protect the confidentiality, integrity, and availability of the system and its information.
Security Impact Analysis	The analysis conducted by an agency official, often during the continuous monitoring phase of the security certification and accreditation process, to determine the extent to which changes to the information system have affected the security posture of the system.
Security Objective	Confidentiality, integrity, or availability.
Security Plan	See System Security Plan.
Security Requirements [CNSS Inst. 4009, Adapted]	Types and levels of protection necessary for equipment, data, information, applications, and facilities to meet laws, Executive Orders, directives, policies, or regulations.
Senior Agency Information Security Officer	Official responsible for carrying out the Chief Information Officer responsibilities under FISMA and serving as the Chief Information Officer's primary liaison to the agency's authorizing officials, information system owners, and information system security officers.
Subsystem	A major subdivision or component of an information system consisting of information, information technology, and personnel that performs one or more specific functions.
System	See Information System.
System-specific Security Control	A security control for an information system that has not been designated as a common security control.
System Security Plan [NIST SP 800-18]	Formal document that provides an overview of the security requirements for the information system and describes the security controls in place or planned for meeting those requirements.
Technical Controls [NIST SP 800-18, Adapted]	The security controls (i.e., safeguards or countermeasures) for an information system that are primarily implemented and executed by the information system through mechanisms contained in the hardware, software, or firmware components of the system.

Threat [CNSS Inst. 4009, Adapted]	Any circumstance or event with the potential to adversely impact agency operations (including mission, functions, image, or reputation), agency assets, or individuals through an information system via unauthorized access, destruction, disclosure, modification of information, and/or denial of service.
Threat Agent	See Threat Source.
Threat Assessment [CNSS Inst. 4009]	Formal description and evaluation of threat to an information system.
Threat Source [NIST SP 800-30]	Either: (i) intent and method targeted at the intentional exploitation of a vulnerability; or (ii) a situation and method that may accidentally trigger a vulnerability. Synonymous with threat agent.
User Representative	An individual that represents the operational interests of the user community and serves as the liaison for that community throughout the system development life cycle of the information system.
Vulnerability [CNSS Inst. 4009, Adapted]	Weakness in an information system, system security procedures, internal controls, or implementation that could be exploited or triggered by a threat source.
Vulnerability Assessment [CNSS Inst. 4009]	Formal description and evaluation of the vulnerabilities in an information system.

APPENDIX C

ACRONYMS
COMMON ABBREVIATIONS

CIO	Chief Information Officer
CNSS	Committee for National Security Systems
COTS	Commercial Off The Shelf
DCID	Director of Central Intelligence Directive
FIPS	Federal Information Processing Standard(s)
FISMA	Federal Information Security Management Act
MOA	Memorandum of Agreement
MOU	Memorandum of Understanding
NIAP	National Information Assurance Partnership
NIST	National Institute of Standards and Technology
NSA	National Security Agency
OMB	Office of Management and Budget
U.S.C.	United States Code

APPENDIX D

SUMMARY OF PHASES AND RESPONSIBILITIES

LISTING BY SECURITY CERTIFICATION AND ACCREDITATION TASK AND SUBTASK

PHASES, TASKS, AND SUBTASKS	RESPONSIBILITY
Initiation Phase	
Task 1: Preparation	
Subtask 1.1: Information System Description	Information System Owner
Subtask 1.2: Security Categorization	Information System Owner
Subtask 1.3: Threat Identification	Information System Owner
Subtask 1.4: Vulnerability Identification	Information System Owner
Subtask 1.5: Security Control Identification	Information System Owner
Subtask 1.6: Initial Risk Determination	Information System Owner
Task 2: Notification and Resource Identification	
Subtask 2.1: Notification	Information System Owner
Subtask 2.2: Planning and Resources	Authorizing Official Senior Agency Information Security Officer Information System Owner Certification Agent
Task 3: System Security Plan Analysis, Update, and Acceptance	
Subtask 3.1: Security Categorization Review	Authorizing Official Senior Agency Information Security Officer Certification Agent
Subtask 3.2: System Security Plan Analysis	Authorizing Official Senior Agency Information Security Officer Certification Agent
Subtask 3.3: System Security Plan Update	Information System Owner
Subtask 3.4: System Security Plan Acceptance	Authorizing Official Senior Agency Information Security Officer
Security Certification Phase	
Task 4: Security Control Assessment	
Subtask 4.1: Documentation and Supporting Materials	Information System Owner Certification Agent
Subtask 4.2: Methods and Procedures	Certification Agent
Subtask 4.3: Security Assessment	Certification Agent
Subtask 4.4: Security Assessment Report	Certification Agent
Task 5: Security Certification Documentation	
Subtask 5.1: Findings and Recommendations	Certification Agent
Subtask 5.2: System Security Plan Update	Information System Owner
Subtask 5.3: Plan of Action and Milestones Preparation	Information System Owner
Subtask 5.4: Accreditation Package Assembly	Information System Owner

PHASES, TASKS, AND SUBTASKS	RESPONSIBILITY
Security Accreditation Phase	
Task 6: Security Accreditation Decision	
Subtask 6.1: Final Risk Determination	Authorizing Official
Subtask 6.2: Risk Acceptability	Authorizing Official
Task 7: Security Accreditation Documentation	
Subtask 7.1: Security Accreditation Package Transmission	Authorizing Official
Subtask 7.2: System Security Plan Update	Information System Owner
Continuous Monitoring Phase	
Task 8: Configuration Management and Control	
Subtask 8.1: Documentation of Information System Changes	Information System Owner
Subtask 8.2: Security Impact Analysis	Information System Owner
Task 9: Security Control Monitoring	
Subtask 9.1: Security Control Selection	Information System Owner
Subtask 9.2: Selected Security Control Assessment	Information System Owner
Task 10: Status Reporting and Documentation	
Subtask 10.1: System Security Plan Update	Information System Owner
Subtask 10.2: Plan of Action and Milestones Update	Information System Owner
Subtask 10.3: Status Reporting	Information System Owner

APPENDIX E

SAMPLE TRANSMITTAL AND DECISION LETTERS
AUTHORIZATION, INTERIM AUTHORIZATION, AND DENIAL OF AUTHORIZATION

Security Accreditation Package Transmittal Letter

From: Information System Owner   Date:

Thru: Senior Agency Information Security Officer

To: Authorizing Official

Subject: Security Accreditation Package for [INFORMATION SYSTEM]

A security certification of the [INFORMATION SYSTEM] and its constituent subsystem-level components (if applicable) located at [LOCATION] has been conducted in accordance with Office of Management and Budget Circular A-130, Appendix III, *Security of Federal Automated Information Resources*; NIST Special Publication 800-37, *Guide for the Security Certification and Accreditation of Federal Information Systems*; and the [AGENCY] policy on security accreditation. The attached security accreditation package contains: (i) current system security plan; (ii) security assessment report; and (iii) plan of action and milestones.

The security controls listed in the system security plan have been assessed by [CERTIFICATION AGENT] using the assessment methods and procedures described in the security assessment report to determine the extent to which the controls are implemented correctly, operating as intended, and producing the desired outcome with respect to meeting the security requirements for the system. The plan of action and milestones describes the corrective measures that have been implemented or are planned to address any deficiencies in the security controls for the information system and to reduce or eliminate known vulnerabilities.

Signature

Title

Enclosures

Security Accreditation Decision Letter (Authorization to Operate)

From: Authorizing Official   Date:

Thru: Senior Agency Information Security Officer

To: Information System Owner

Subject: Security Accreditation Decision for [INFORMATION SYSTEM]

After reviewing the results of the security certification of the [INFORMATION SYSTEM] and its constituent system-level components (if applicable) located at [LOCATION] and the supporting evidence provided in the associated security accreditation package (including the current system security plan, the security assessment report, and the plan of action and milestones), I have determined that the risk to agency operations, agency assets, or individuals resulting from the operation of the information system is acceptable. Accordingly, I am issuing an *authorization to operate* the information system in its existing operating environment. The information system is accredited without any significant restrictions or limitations. This security accreditation is my formal declaration that adequate security controls have been implemented in the information system and that a satisfactory level of security is present in the system.

The security accreditation of the information system will remain in effect as long as: (i) the required security status reports for the system are submitted to this office every [TIME PERIOD]; (ii) the vulnerabilities reported during the continuous monitoring process do not result in additional agency-level risk which is deemed unacceptable; and (iii) the system has not exceeded the maximum allowable time period between security accreditations in accordance with federal or agency policy.

A copy of this letter with all supporting security certification and accreditation documentation should be retained in accordance with the agency's record retention schedule.

Signature

Title

Enclosures

Security Accreditation Decision Letter (Interim Authorization to Operate)

From: Authorizing Official   Date:

Thru: Senior Agency Information Security Officer

To: Information System Owner

Subject: Security Accreditation Decision for [INFORMATION SYSTEM]

After reviewing the results of the security certification of the [INFORMATION SYSTEM] and its constituent system-level components (if applicable) located at [LOCATION] and the supporting evidence provided in the associated security accreditation package (including the current system security plan, the security assessment report, and the plan of action and milestones), I have determined that the risk to agency operations, agency assets, or individuals resulting from the operation of the information system is *not* acceptable. However, I have also determined that there is an overarching need to place the information system into operation or continue its operation due to mission necessity. Accordingly, I am issuing an *interim authorization to operate* the information system in its existing operating environment. An interim authorization is a limited authorization to operate the information system under specific terms and conditions and acknowledges greater agency-level risk for a limited period of time. The information system is *not* considered accredited during the period of limited authorization to operate. The terms and conditions of this limited authorization are described in Attachment A.

A process must be established immediately to monitor the effectiveness of the security controls in the information system during the period of limited authorization. Monitoring activities should focus on the specific areas of concern identified during the security certification. Significant changes in the security state of the information system during the period of limited authorization should be reported immediately.

This interim authorization to operate the information system is valid for [TIME PERIOD]. The limited authorization will remain in effect during that time period as long as: (i) the required security status reports for the system are submitted to this office every [TIME PERIOD]; (ii) the vulnerabilities reported during the continuous monitoring process do not result in additional agency-level risk which is deemed unacceptable; and (iii) continued progress is being made in reducing or eliminating vulnerabilities in the information system in accordance with the plan of action and milestones. At the end of the period of limited authorization, the information system must be either authorized to operate or the authorization for further operation will be denied. Renewals or extensions to this interim authorization to operate will be granted only under the most extenuating of circumstances. This office will monitor the plan of action and milestones submitted with the accreditation package during the period of limited authorization.

A copy of this letter with all supporting security certification and accreditation documentation should be retained in accordance with the agency's record retention schedule.

Signature

Title

Enclosures

Security Accreditation Decision Letter (Denial of Authorization to Operate)

From: Authorizing Official   Date:

Thru: Senior Agency Information Security Officer

To: Information System Owner

Subject: Security Accreditation Decision for [INFORMATION SYSTEM]

After reviewing the results of the security certification of the [INFORMATION SYSTEM] and its constituent system-level components (if applicable) located at [LOCATION] and the supporting evidence provided in the associated security accreditation package (including the current system security plan, the security assessment report, and the plan of action and milestones), I have determined that the risk to agency operations, agency assets, or individuals resulting from the operation of the information system is unacceptable. Accordingly, I am issuing a denial of authorization to operate the information system in its existing operating environment. The information system is *not* accredited and [MAY NOT BE PLACED INTO OPERATION or ALL CURRENT OPERATIONS MUST BE HALTED]. Failure to receive an authorization to operate the information system indicates that there are major deficiencies in the security controls in the system and that a satisfactory level of security is not present in the system at this time.

The plan of action and milestones should be revised immediately to ensure that proactive measures are taken to correct the security deficiencies in the information system. The security certification should be repeated at the earliest opportunity to determine the effectiveness of the security controls in the information system after the reduction or elimination of identified vulnerabilities.

A copy of this letter with all supporting security certification and accreditation documentation should be retained in accordance with the agency's record retention schedule.

Signature

Title

Enclosures